History of Fashion Step by Step

Fashion Through the Ages: Trends, Icons & Movements

Lydia Ford

© 2024 by Lydia Ford

All rights reserved.

No part of this publication may be reproduced, distributed, or transmitted in any form or by any means, including photocopying, recording, or other electronic or mechanical methods, without the prior written permission of the publisher, except in the case of brief quotations embodied in critical reviews and certain other noncommercial uses permitted by U.S. copyright law.

This book is intended to provide general information on the subjects covered and is presented with the understanding that the author and publisher are not providing professional advice or services. While every effort has been made to ensure the accuracy and completeness of the information contained herein, neither the author nor the publisher guarantees such accuracy or completeness, nor shall they be responsible for any errors or omissions or for the results obtained from the use of such information. The contents of this book are provided "as is" and without warranties of any kind, either express or implied.

Publisher email: info@tagvault.org

PREFACE

Fashion is far more than fabric and stitches—it's a mirror reflecting human history, culture, and society. Every era has used clothing to tell stories, assert power, challenge norms, and express individuality. From the flowing tunics of ancient Greece to the daring streetwear of today, fashion has always been a creative outlet and a way to communicate without words.

History of Fashion Step by Step was born from a love of this dynamic, ever-changing world of style. The goal of this book is simple: to go on a journey through the ages, unraveling the threads of how fashion has evolved, and to understand what it reveals about the people and times it comes from. This book doesn't just chronicle the hemlines and silhouettes; it goes deeper, exploring the cultural, economic, and technological shifts that have shaped what we wear.

Fashion is an extraordinary lens through which to view history. It has influenced revolutions, represented freedom, and challenged social hierarchies. What we choose to wear—or are told to wear—reflects our values, status, and aspirations. From the luxurious courts of Louis XIV to the unpretentious yet bold grunge movement of the 1990s, clothing has acted as both an artistic medium and a societal marker.

This book is designed to be accessible, engaging, and thorough. It's not just for fashion enthusiasts or historians; it's for anyone curious about the stories behind what we wear. Whether you're a student, a creative professional, or simply someone who has wondered why fashion seems to repeat itself, this book offers a clear and comprehensive look at the topic.

We start with the very origins of clothing—how humans first began to use textiles for protection and expression. From there, we go into the vibrant world of antiquity, where garments were deeply tied to cultural identity. You'll see how the opulence of the Baroque period gave way to the restrained elegance of the Neoclassical era and how industrialization revolutionized the way clothing was made and consumed.

Fashion is, by nature, cyclical, and this book explores why. The trends we see today are often echoes of the past, reinvented for modern sensibilities. For example, the 1970s fascination with ethnic-inspired clothing mirrored the global exploration and cultural blending seen in earlier centuries. Similarly, the rise of sustainable fashion recalls earlier periods when garments were carefully crafted to last, rather than being discarded after a single season.

One of the most exciting parts of fashion history is how it reflects shifts in power. Clothing has been used to signal status, but it has also been wielded as a tool for rebellion. Think of the punk movement's ripped jeans and safety pins—deliberately rejecting the polished looks of the mainstream—or the French Revolution's move away from the elaborate costumes of the aristocracy toward simpler, utilitarian styles. Fashion is never just about aesthetics. It's intertwined with the political and social climates of its time.

This book also embraces the future. The last chapter looks ahead to where fashion might be going. With innovations in technology and a growing emphasis on sustainability, we're entering an era where fashion might not only change how we look but also how we interact with the world around us. Smart textiles, virtual fashion, and ethical manufacturing are just some of the exciting possibilities shaping the industry today.

Throughout this journey, I've tried to strike a balance between being informative and approachable. Each chapter builds on the one before it, creating a step-by-step path through history. At the same time, I've included fascinating anecdotes and cultural insights to keep things lively and engaging.

At the end of the book, you'll find an appendix with terms and definitions to clarify key concepts and a timeline of major fashion moments for easy reference. My hope is that this structure makes the book as practical as it is enjoyable to read.

So, whether you're opening this book to gain inspiration for your own style, deepen your understanding of history, or simply satisfy your curiosity, I welcome you. Fashion is a journey, and I'm thrilled to have you here to explore it, step by step.

TOPICAL OUTLINE

Chapter 1: The Essence of Fashion
- The Origins of Clothing
- Fashion as Identity
- Fashion in Rituals and Ceremonies
- The Role of Textiles
- Fashion and Power
- The Spread of Style
- Why Fashion is Cyclical
- The Philosophy of Fashion

Chapter 2: Fashion in Antiquity
- Egyptian Elegance
- Greek Drapery
- Roman Innovations
- Persian and Eastern Influences

Chapter 3: Medieval Modes
- The Influence of the Church
- Sumptuary Laws and Class Distinction
- The Rise of Tailoring

Chapter 4: Renaissance Revival
- The Rebirth of Luxury Fabrics
- Gendered Styles in Renaissance Europe
- The Spread of Italian and French Influence

Chapter 5: Baroque and Rococo Opulence
- Extravagance in the Court of Louis XIV
- Rococo Elegance and Ornamentation
- The Role of Accessories
- The Birth of Fashion Icons in Royal Courts

Chapter 6: Revolutionary Simplicity
- The Impact of the French Revolution on Dress
- Neoclassicism and the Empire Silhouette
- The Democratization of Fashion

Chapter 7: The Victorian Era
- Crinolines and Corsets
- Mourning Dress and Social Codes
- Industrialization and Mass Production

Chapter 8: The Birth of Modern Fashion
- The Rise of Haute Couture
- The House of Worth
- The Role of Fashion Magazines
- The Influence of the Belle Époque on Fashion

Chapter 9: The Early 20th Century
- The Influence of World Wars on Fashion
- The Advent of Ready-to-Wear
- Flapper Fashion and the Roaring Twenties
- Art Deco and Modernist Movements

Chapter 10: Mid-Century Fashion
- Dior's New Look
- Post-War Innovation
- The Role of Hollywood in Fashion
- The Impact of Global Events on Design Trends

Chapter 11: The Counterculture Sixties
- The Rise of Youth Culture
- Mod Fashion and Mary Quant
- The Influence of Music and Pop Art

Chapter 12: The 1970s: Individualism and Expression
- Hippie Style and Counterculture
- Disco Glamour
- Punk Fashion
- Ethnic Revival and Global Inspirations

Chapter 13: The Power Dressing of the 1980s
- Shoulder Pads and Corporate Looks
- The Influence of Supermodels
- Sportswear and Street Style

Chapter 14: The Minimalism of the 1990s
- Grunge Fashion
- The Influence of Designers Like Calvin Klein
- Globalization of Fashion Brands

Chapter 15: 21st-Century Fashion Trends
- Sustainability and Ethical Fashion
- The Rise of Fast Fashion
- Digital and Influencer Impact on Style
- The Intersection of Gender Neutrality and Style

Chapter 16: The Future of Fashion
- Technological Innovations in Fabric and Design
- The Role of AI and Virtual Fashion
- Predictions for Emerging Trends

Appendix
- Timeline of Major Fashion Moments Through History
- Terms and Definitions

TABLE OF CONTENTS

Chapter 1: The Essence of Fashion ... 1
Chapter 2: Fashion in Antiquity ... 19
Chapter 3: Medieval Modes ... 30
Chapter 4: Renaissance Revival ... 37
Chapter 5: Baroque and Rococo Opulence ... 43
Chapter 6: Revolutionary Simplicity ... 51
Chapter 7: The Victorian Era ... 57
Chapter 8: The Birth of Modern Fashion ... 63
Chapter 9: The Early 20th Century ... 72
Chapter 10: Mid-Century Fashion ... 82
Chapter 11: The Counterculture Sixties ... 91
Chapter 12: The 1970s: Individualism and Expression ... 97
Chapter 13: The Power Dressing of the 1980s ... 106
Chapter 14: The Minimalism of the 1990s ... 112
Chapter 15: 21st-Century Fashion Trends ... 118
Chapter 16: The Future of Fashion ... 127
Appendix ... 133
Afterword ... 140

CHAPTER 1: THE ESSENCE OF FASHION

The Origins of Clothing

Clothing began as a necessity, not a statement. Early humans needed protection from harsh climates, sharp rocks, and biting insects. Evidence of this is found in prehistoric tools: scrapers, awls, and needles made from bone, indicating that as far back as 100,000 years ago, humans were making basic garments. These were likely animal hides softened with fat and sewn together using sinew. Such clothing wasn't decorative—it was survival gear.

The first evidence of textiles dates back to around 36,000 years ago, found in caves in what is now the Czech Republic. Here, impressions of woven fibers were discovered on clay fragments, showing that humans were experimenting with weaving long before agriculture. These early textiles were likely plant-based, made from flax or grasses. Flax fibers, found in caves in Georgia and dated to around 30,000 years ago, show that humans spun fibers into threads. This development was monumental because woven fabric offered flexibility and comfort, a leap forward from stiff animal skins.

Animal skins, however, dominated clothing for thousands of years. Early humans developed sophisticated ways to process hides. Tanning, for instance, was practiced by Neanderthals and early Homo sapiens. By treating the hides with fats or plant tannins, they made leather that was durable and water-resistant. Fur was particularly prized in cold climates. Arctic and sub-Arctic communities crafted sophisticated garments using layered animal skins, stitching them with incredible precision using bone needles. These techniques ensured survival in some of the harshest environments on Earth.

Clothing was also shaped by migration. When humans began to leave Africa around 70,000 years ago, they entered regions where climate demanded innovation. In colder regions, layered clothing became necessary. In warmer areas, lightweight coverings shielded the body from the sun. Archaeological evidence suggests that cultural exchange likely accelerated during these migrations. Tools, techniques, and ideas for clothing spread and evolved as groups encountered one another.

Symbolism in early clothing emerged surprisingly early. Around 75,000 years ago, in Blombos Cave, South Africa, perforated shells were discovered that had been strung into necklaces. These weren't strictly clothing, but they suggest that humans were already adorning themselves for reasons beyond utility. Beads and adornments would later influence clothing design, as the desire for self-expression became intertwined with necessity.

By 10,000 BCE, as agriculture took hold during the Neolithic period, clothing saw dramatic changes. The domestication of sheep and goats provided wool, while plants like flax were cultivated for linen. This marked the beginning of textiles as a controlled craft. Spinning fibers into yarn and weaving them into fabric became common. The spinning wheel didn't yet exist, but humans used simple tools like spindles and looms. Early looms were rudimentary—horizontal wooden frames with strings stretched across to form a warp. Weavers would thread the weft through by hand, creating plain but functional cloth.

Regional variations in materials and techniques developed rapidly. In the Fertile Crescent, linen dominated due to abundant flax, while in China, silk emerged as a revolutionary textile. The Chinese learned to harvest silk threads from the cocoons of silkworms as early as 3,000 BCE, though legend credits its discovery to the wife of Emperor Huangdi. This lightweight, shimmering fabric had no parallel in the ancient world, and its production was kept secret for centuries, giving rise to the lucrative Silk Road trade.

In other parts of the world, early cultures adapted to their environments. In Central and South America, cotton became a primary material. Cotton plants thrived in tropical climates, and archaeological evidence shows that Mesoamerican peoples wove cotton fabric as early as 5,000 BCE. Meanwhile, in the Arctic, Inuit and Yupik peoples crafted ingenious garments from caribou skin and sealskin, which provided insulation even in sub-zero temperatures. These garments were not just functional; they were tailored with astonishing precision to reduce heat loss.

Around the same time, technological advancements began influencing clothing. The invention of the needle transformed garment-making. By allowing precise stitching, it enabled humans to create fitted clothing rather than simple draped garments. A fitted tunic or coat retained body heat more effectively and allowed greater freedom of movement, critical for hunting and daily survival. Early needles made of bone, antler, and later metal allowed for remarkable advances in craftsmanship.

Cultural factors began to shape clothing more distinctively during this period. With the rise of agricultural societies, humans no longer needed to move constantly in search of food, and clothing began to reflect community identity. Decoration became more common, with dyes made from plants, insects, and minerals adding color to garments. Red ochre, indigo, and woad are some of the earliest known dyes, used to create earthy reds, deep blues, and vibrant yellows. Patterns were also introduced, often symbolizing tribal affiliation or social status.

Trade brought further innovation. As early as 3,000 BCE, civilizations such as the Mesopotamians, Egyptians, and Indus Valley peoples traded textiles along with other goods. This exchange introduced new materials and techniques to different regions. For example, Egyptian linen was highly prized throughout the ancient world, while Babylonian merchants traded intricately embroidered textiles.

Religious practices influenced early clothing. In Egypt, priests wore linen garments to signify purity, while in Mesopotamia, ceremonial robes were adorned with symbolic patterns. Clothing also denoted rank: in many societies, rulers and elites dressed differently from commoners, signaling their status through materials and embellishments. This distinction would grow even more pronounced in later centuries with the introduction of sumptuary laws.

The **transition from necessity to artistry** was gradual but unmistakable. By the Bronze Age (around 3,300 BCE), clothing reflected technological advances, cultural identities, and individual creativity. Decorative techniques like embroidery, appliqué, and pleating began to appear. These required time and skill, making them available only to those of higher status. Even then, the aesthetic element of clothing became increasingly significant.

Leatherworking also continued to evolve during this time. The Hittites and other early civilizations became experts in crafting leather footwear, belts, and armor. Leather sandals, for instance, were common in Egypt, while more sophisticated boots appeared in colder regions. These advancements show how adaptable early humans were in meeting environmental challenges while enhancing the functionality of their clothing.

Head coverings and accessories, which would later become defining aspects of fashion, also began to take shape in the earliest clothing traditions. Hats made from straw, fur, or leather offered protection from the sun and cold while signaling roles within a community. For example, the **Ötzi the Iceman**, a naturally mummified man from around 3,300 BCE, was discovered wearing a fur hat that provided warmth in the Alps, where he likely lived.

By the time written records appeared, clothing had already become a defining feature of human culture. Ancient Sumerian tablets describe garments made of wool, while Egyptian hieroglyphs show elaborate linen outfits worn by pharaohs and nobles. These records reveal a shift: clothing was no longer just practical but symbolic, a reflection of the wearer's role, wealth, and even morality.

The origins of clothing underscore humanity's ingenuity. Early garments were not just about covering the body but responding to specific needs—survival, comfort, identity, and status. They tell us about the environments people lived in, the challenges they faced, and the creative solutions they developed to thrive.

Fashion as Identity

Fashion has always been a powerful expression of identity. From the earliest human societies, clothing served as more than mere protection. It signified who you were, where you came from, and what you valued. By altering materials, colors, and styles, individuals and groups communicated their roles and affiliations without words. **Clothing became a visual language, one that evolved alongside humanity itself.**

In ancient societies, clothing differentiated tribes and marked social hierarchies. Patterns, embellishments, and colors often carried symbolic meanings. For example, in early Mesopotamian cultures, clothing made of wool and flax indicated a person's economic standing. Wealthier individuals wore garments dyed in rare colors, such as deep blue or red, made from labor-intensive processes using indigo or crushed insects like cochineal. In contrast, commoners wore simpler, undyed materials. These visual distinctions were unmistakable and reinforced social structure at a glance.

Cultural identity was closely tied to regional materials and techniques. In ancient Egypt, lightweight linen clothing was not only practical for the climate but also symbolic of purity and spirituality. The quality and transparency of the fabric reflected a person's status—sheer linen was often reserved for the elite. Similarly, the Celts of Europe wore tartans and plaids woven with specific patterns that identified their clans. These patterns, painstakingly crafted on simple looms, acted as a badge of heritage, tying people to their ancestry.

Gender identity was often signaled through clothing, with distinctions in style and decoration emerging in almost every culture. Ancient Greek men and women both wore draped garments such as chitons and himations, but the length and ornamentation varied by gender. Men's clothing was shorter and simpler, designed for physical activity and public life, while women's garments were longer, often adorned with intricate embroidery to reflect domestic roles and modesty ideals. These conventions, though culturally specific, served as clear markers of societal expectations.

Fashion also expressed marital and familial identity. In ancient Rome, married women wore a specific garment called the stola, a long, sleeveless tunic worn over an underdress. This garment not only distinguished married women from unmarried ones but also highlighted their adherence to Roman virtues of modesty and respectability. Similarly, in traditional Japanese culture, the kimono's design, color, and pattern often reflected the wearer's marital status or family affiliations, with certain motifs and hues reserved for specific life stages.

Religious identity shaped clothing choices as well. For centuries, Jewish men wore fringed garments (tzitzit) as a sign of adherence to religious commandments, while Christian monks donned simple robes to demonstrate humility and devotion. In Islam, modest dress, such as the hijab or abaya, communicates faith and community belonging. These garments are not merely utilitarian; they are infused with meaning, connecting the individual to a greater spiritual or cultural collective.

Fashion also evolved as a means of asserting individuality within group identities. Renaissance Europe saw a rise in personal tailoring and accessorizing among the upper classes. Individuals expressed themselves through detailed embroidery, imported fabrics, and lavish embellishments. While certain trends and silhouettes dictated broader societal norms, the details allowed for personal flair. A lace collar, a silk sash, or a carefully chosen jewel could signal wealth, taste, and even intellectual leanings.

In modern contexts, clothing still functions as a marker of identity. Subcultures, such as punk in the 1970s or hip-hop in the 1980s, developed distinct styles to challenge societal norms and celebrate their uniqueness. Punk fashion rejected polished aesthetics with ripped jeans, safety pins, and DIY embellishments, while hip-hop adopted oversized clothing, bold logos, and flashy accessories to assert a defiant, urban identity. These movements demonstrate how fashion can empower individuals to claim space within or outside of societal frameworks.

Even today, uniforms remain a powerful expression of identity. Police officers, doctors, and soldiers wear standardized clothing that immediately conveys their roles and responsibilities. In schools, uniforms can represent unity and discipline while also marking socioeconomic divides, as students from wealthier families often distinguish themselves with branded shoes or accessories.

Clothing continues to reflect shifting identities in our globalized world. Gender-neutral fashion challenges traditional binaries, creating space for self-expression beyond conventional expectations. Sustainability movements have also influenced identity, with many consumers choosing thrifted or ethically made clothing to reflect their environmental values. In these cases, fashion is not just about aesthetics but about signaling deeply held beliefs.

Ultimately, fashion as identity remains a dynamic, evolving concept. It adapts to cultural shifts, personal choices, and societal pressures, constantly renegotiating what it means to belong, to stand out, and to be seen.

Fashion in Rituals and Ceremonies

Clothing has been an essential component of rituals and ceremonies across cultures and epochs. It goes beyond aesthetics or practicality, serving as a vessel for meaning, belief, and tradition. **In ceremonies, every stitch, color, and accessory can carry layers of symbolism, linking the individual to their community, ancestors, or spiritual beliefs.**

One of the earliest recorded uses of ceremonial clothing comes from ancient Egypt. Pharaohs wore heavily adorned garments for religious rites, often made of fine linen and decorated with gold thread and semi-precious stones. These garments symbolized their divine connection and authority. The nemes headdress, with its striped cloth and uraeus (a cobra emblem), was not only a practical sun shield but also a statement of power and protection. The ankh motif, often embroidered into royal clothing, reinforced themes of eternal life and divine favor.

In indigenous African cultures, ceremonial clothing often included elaborate beadwork, each pattern and color holding specific meanings. Among the Zulu, beadwork on clothing communicates messages about the wearer's marital status, age, and family connections. For example, in a wedding ceremony, a Zulu bride's isidwaba (traditional skirt) and beaded necklaces are created with patterns chosen to honor her ancestors and symbolize her transition to womanhood.

Religious rituals frequently dictated strict dress codes. In ancient Mesopotamia, priests wore robes made from specific materials, such as wool, dyed purple or white to signify purity or connection to the divine. In India, Hindu ceremonies incorporated saffron-colored clothing, which represents purity and spirituality. Brides in Hindu weddings traditionally wear red saris, chosen for their association with prosperity and fertility, while white is reserved for mourning ceremonies.

The clothing used in mourning ceremonies often communicates collective grief and respect for the departed. In ancient Rome, mourners wore dark, unadorned togas, contrasting with the elaborate clothing typically seen at public events. During the Victorian era, elaborate mourning dress became codified, with strict rules dictating the fabrics, colors, and duration of wearing black. Widows wore heavy black crepe for months or even years, symbolizing their enduring grief.

Weddings have historically been among the most elaborate ceremonies, with clothing serving as a focal point. In medieval Europe, brides often wore their best dress, regardless of color, as a statement of their family's wealth and social standing. White only became a popular choice after Queen Victoria's wedding in 1840, where her white silk gown set a trend that endures in Western culture. In China, by contrast, red has been the traditional wedding color for centuries, symbolizing joy, luck, and fertility. Modern Chinese weddings often blend these traditions, with brides wearing a red qipao during the ceremony and a Western-style white dress for the reception.

Initiation ceremonies also feature highly symbolic clothing. In coming-of-age rituals across many African tribes, young men or women undergoing rites of passage often wear distinctive garments crafted by their families or community elders. Among the Maasai, young warriors wear red shukas (cloth wraps) as they transition into adulthood, a color representing strength and bravery.

Across indigenous cultures in the Americas, ceremonial clothing reflects deep spiritual connections to nature. Native American regalia, worn during powwows or sacred dances, is handcrafted with feathers, beads, and leather, each element chosen for its cultural significance. The Plains tribes, for instance, use eagle feathers in headdresses to symbolize strength and vision, while beadwork patterns honor specific ancestors or spirits.

Festivals also demand ceremonial dress. During Japan's Shinto festivals, participants wear yukata (light cotton kimonos) adorned with motifs tied to the season or the shrine being celebrated. Similarly, in Hindu festivals like Diwali, vibrant, newly purchased clothing signifies renewal and prosperity, reinforcing the celebration's themes.

Political ceremonies have long used clothing to assert authority and continuity. Coronation robes, such as those worn by European monarchs, are embroidered with gold and adorned with symbols like lions, fleur-de-lis, or crosses, signifying divine approval and national pride. The heavy velvet and fur garments worn during these occasions emphasize permanence and tradition.

Modern rituals, from graduations to inaugurations, continue the tradition of symbolic clothing. Caps and gowns at graduations trace back to medieval academic robes, signaling the wearer's scholarly achievement. Inauguration suits or dresses often reflect cultural or national pride, blending modern fashion with traditional motifs.

Clothing in rituals and ceremonies tells stories, binds communities, and bridges the human and the divine. Each piece, carefully crafted and worn, resonates with meaning, capturing the essence of what it means to participate in a collective tradition.

The Role of Textiles

Textiles are the backbone of fashion. Long before modern design and tailoring, textiles determined what people could wear and how they expressed themselves. A textile's availability, durability, and adaptability dictated its importance, and the techniques used to produce it reveal much about human innovation and society's priorities.

The earliest textiles were made from natural materials such as animal hides, plant fibers, and tree bark. Ancient humans in regions rich in flax plants spun and wove this fiber into linen. Flax fibers unearthed in caves in the Caucasus, dating back 30,000 years, are among the oldest evidence of this process. Linen was prized for its durability and ability to keep the body cool, making it ideal for the climates of Mesopotamia and Egypt. Wool, meanwhile, became a staple textile in colder regions. The domestication of sheep around 8,000 BCE ensured a steady supply of this insulating material, and its elasticity made it easy to spin into yarn.

Textile production became one of the earliest industries, with complex processes developing to prepare, dye, and weave materials. By 2,000 BCE, Mesopotamians used vertical looms to produce elaborate textiles. These were labor-intensive creations, often requiring months to complete. The introduction of dyes from natural sources such as plants, insects, and minerals added another layer of complexity. The indigo plant, native to India, became a major source of deep blue dye, while madder roots were used to create vibrant reds. These colors were more than aesthetic—they were social markers, as dyed fabrics were costly and laborious to produce.

Silk, discovered in China around 3,000 BCE, revolutionized textiles. This lightweight, lustrous material came from the cocoons of the silkworm, a labor-intensive process requiring careful harvesting and spinning. Silk's fine texture and shimmering quality made it a luxury good, reserved for elites and used as currency in trade. The secrecy surrounding silk production for centuries amplified its mystique, and the Silk Road trade routes helped spread this coveted textile across continents.

Cotton, another transformative textile, was cultivated independently in regions like the Indus Valley, South America, and Africa. Its softness, breathability, and versatility made it a favorite material in warmer climates. By 3,000 BCE, cotton was being spun and woven into cloth in India, where advanced techniques allowed for the creation of muslin, a fine, sheer fabric that would later captivate European traders.

The mechanization of textile production began in earnest during the 18th century, but even before the Industrial Revolution, tools like the spinning wheel had already transformed efficiency. These advancements made textiles more widely available, which in turn influenced fashion. As production increased, textiles became more varied. Velvet, satin, and brocade emerged, offering designers more options for creativity and self-expression.

Different societies developed textiles unique to their environments and needs. The Navajo in North America wove intricate wool rugs and garments, while the Andean peoples crafted textiles from alpaca and llama fibers, creating vibrant designs rich in symbolism. In West Africa, strip-weaving techniques produced kente cloth, a fabric imbued with cultural and spiritual meaning.

Throughout history, textiles have shaped economies. For instance, the European demand for Indian cotton and Chinese silk drove trade empires and colonization. The rise of the transatlantic slave trade was tied directly to the production of textiles, as enslaved Africans were forced to labor on cotton plantations in the Americas. Textiles were not only commodities; they were central to global power structures.

Textiles also influenced technological innovation. Inventions such as the Jacquard loom in the 19th century automated complex weaving patterns, laying the groundwork for computer programming concepts. Even today, the study of textiles continues to push boundaries, from the development of smart fabrics to the creation of sustainable alternatives like bamboo and hemp.

The story of textiles is one of resilience, adaptability, and ingenuity. It has shaped how people dress, live, and interact with the world around them.

Fashion and Power

Fashion and power have been intertwined since the earliest civilizations. Clothing has always served as a visual indicator of authority, wealth, and influence, often used to enforce hierarchies or challenge them. The ability to control fashion—or be excluded from it—has frequently reflected broader struggles for dominance and autonomy.

In ancient societies, power was often displayed through the exclusivity of materials and dyes. Egyptian pharaohs, for example, wore intricately designed garments made from the finest linen, adorned with gold thread and beaded collars. Their clothing not only symbolized divine authority but also reminded subjects of the ruler's access to rare resources. Gold and lapis lazuli, incorporated into ceremonial attire, reinforced the perception of eternal, godlike power.

Dyes carried immense political and economic weight. Purple, derived from the mucus of sea snails, was one of the rarest and most expensive dyes in antiquity. The Phoenicians, who monopolized its production, used it to dye the robes of royalty. The Roman Empire went so far as to restrict the use of Tyrian purple through sumptuary laws, ensuring only emperors and high-ranking officials could wear it. Violating these laws was seen as a challenge to imperial authority, demonstrating how tightly clothing was controlled to maintain power structures.

Clothing was also used to signal allegiance or rebellion. In medieval Europe, knights wore surcoats bearing their lord's emblem, visually asserting loyalty on the battlefield. Conversely, during the French Revolution, clothing became a means of defiance. Revolutionaries rejected the elaborate silks and brocades of the aristocracy in favor of simple, utilitarian garments. The sans-culottes, literally "without breeches," became a symbol of the working class, opposing the knee-length breeches worn by the elite. These sartorial choices went beyond practicality—they embodied a rejection of oppression and a call for equality.

Sumptuary laws, which regulated what individuals could wear based on their class or occupation, were common across cultures. In Ming Dynasty China, for example, only the emperor and his immediate family could wear robes embroidered with dragons. Similarly, in medieval England, laws restricted the use of fur trims and specific colors to the nobility. These rules weren't merely about clothing; they reinforced societal boundaries and ensured that visual markers of power remained exclusive.

Religious institutions also wielded power through fashion. Clergy in medieval Europe wore opulent robes made from expensive fabrics, often embroidered with gold and jewels. These garments distinguished religious leaders from laypeople, emphasizing their authority. In contrast, monks wore plain, unadorned robes to symbolize humility, creating a deliberate visual contrast to secular leaders.

Colonial powers used fashion as a tool of domination. European colonizers imposed Western dress codes on indigenous populations, often banning traditional garments. This forced assimilation eroded cultural identities while signaling the colonizer's control. For example, in 19th-century India, British authorities discouraged traditional dhotis and saris in favor of European-style suits and dresses, framing local clothing as "backward." However, resistance movements often reclaimed traditional dress as a symbol of defiance. Mahatma Gandhi's adoption of the simple khadi cloth during India's independence struggle rejected British textiles and emphasized self-reliance.

Fashion's association with power extends to gender dynamics. Historically, women's clothing was often designed to restrict movement, reinforcing social constraints. Corsets in the 19th century reshaped women's bodies into exaggerated silhouettes, reflecting societal ideals of beauty and passivity. Meanwhile, men's fashion evolved toward practicality and authority, with tailored suits dominating professional and political spaces. The shift toward women adopting suits in the early 20th century, popularized by figures like Coco Chanel and Marlene Dietrich, signaled a challenge to traditional gender roles and an assertion of autonomy.

The 20th century saw mass movements harness fashion to assert power. The Black Panther Party in the 1960s adopted a distinctive uniform of leather jackets, berets, and dark sunglasses. This cohesive look not only unified members but projected strength and defiance. Similarly, LGBTQ+ communities used fashion to signal identity and solidarity. The rise of drag culture, for instance, celebrated flamboyant styles as a rebellion against heteronormative expectations.

Modern power dynamics continue to play out in fashion. Political leaders use clothing to shape their public image. Figures like Margaret Thatcher and Angela Merkel adopted tailored, neutral-toned suits to project authority in male-dominated spaces, while others, such as Michelle Obama, blended high fashion with accessibility to appeal to a broader audience. Even today, fast fashion serves as a symbol of economic inequality, with luxury brands maintaining exclusivity while mass-produced imitations cater to the majority.

Fashion remains an arena where power is negotiated and contested. It reflects who holds influence, who seeks to challenge it, and how those dynamics evolve.

The Spread of Style

The spread of style is as old as human interaction itself. From the earliest migrations, as people moved across regions, they carried not only tools and language but also ideas about clothing and ornamentation. Trade, conquest, and cultural exchange accelerated the dissemination of styles, turning clothing into a dynamic medium of interaction and transformation.

One of the earliest examples of style spreading through trade comes from the Silk Road. Dating back to around 130 BCE, this vast network of trade routes connected China, Central Asia, the Middle East, and Europe. Chinese silk, a luxurious fabric unknown in the West, became a highly coveted commodity among Roman elites. By the 1st century CE, Roman aristocrats wore silk imported from China, and this exotic fabric became a symbol of wealth and sophistication. The Silk Road didn't just transport textiles—it carried weaving techniques, dyeing practices, and design motifs, shaping local traditions as it wove cultures together.

The Persian Empire was influential in the spread of styles in antiquity. Located at the crossroads of major trade routes, Persia absorbed influences from India, Greece, and Mesopotamia. Persian garments, such as the kandys—a type of coat worn over the shoulders—were adopted by neighboring cultures, including the Greeks. This exchange was mutual; during the reign of Alexander the Great, Persian influences on Greek clothing grew prominent, resulting in hybrid styles that blended the draped elegance of Greek attire with the tailored construction of Persian garments.

Conquest often spread styles in ways trade could not. When the Mongol Empire expanded across Eurasia in the 13th and 14th centuries, it connected diverse cultures under a single dominion. Mongol rulers embraced and promoted silk garments, and their court became a melting pot of styles from China, Persia, and the Middle East. This amalgamation influenced the clothing traditions of the regions under Mongol control, blending embroidery techniques and fabric patterns into local dress codes.

Religious movements also facilitated the spread of fashion. The Islamic Caliphates, beginning in the 7th century, expanded rapidly across the Middle East, North Africa, and parts of Europe. Islamic culture introduced innovations in textiles, such as intricate brocades and vibrant dyes, to regions as far afield as Spain and India. In return, Islamic artisans adopted elements of Byzantine and Persian styles, incorporating them into their own clothing traditions. For example, the Andalusian region of Spain became famous for its silk-weaving techniques, which were influenced by both Islamic and Christian artisanship.

The Crusades in the medieval period provided another vector for the exchange of styles. Crusaders returning to Europe from the Middle East brought back more than religious relics—they introduced new materials, patterns, and tailoring techniques. European fashion absorbed elements such as flowing robes, rich velvets, and geometric motifs, which had origins in Middle Eastern design. These influences were evident in the luxurious garments worn by European nobility in the 12th and 13th centuries.

Exploration and colonization in the 15th and 16th centuries radically expanded the reach of fashion. Portuguese and Spanish explorers brought textiles like Indian cotton and Chinese silk to Europe. These fabrics revolutionized European wardrobes, offering lightweight, colorful alternatives to traditional wool and linen. The introduction of new dyes, such as cochineal red from the Americas, transformed the color palette of European fashion. Cochineal, derived from insects native to Mexico, produced an intense crimson that became a status symbol among European elites.

The Age of Enlightenment in the 18th century saw style spreading through diplomacy and cultural exchange. French fashion dominated Europe, largely thanks to the influence of Louis XIV's court at Versailles. French tailors and dressmakers set the standard for elegance, and their designs were eagerly copied across the continent. The spread of French fashion wasn't purely organic; it was actively promoted through diplomacy. French textiles, particularly silk from Lyon, were gifted to foreign courts, establishing France as the epicenter of style.

The Industrial Revolution in the 19th century marked a turning point in the dissemination of fashion. Advances in textile manufacturing and transportation made clothing more accessible than ever before. Factories produced garments in bulk, and railways and steamships transported them quickly across regions. Fashion magazines, which began to flourish during this era, spread trends even further, providing readers with detailed illustrations of the latest styles from Paris, London, and New York. Suddenly, people who had never traveled could adopt trends from distant cities.

Mass production also allowed styles from different social classes to intermingle. What had once been the preserve of the aristocracy—fitted jackets, silk cravats, or tailored dresses—became available to the burgeoning middle class. The democratization of fashion didn't erase social distinctions but blurred them, as lower classes adopted and adapted elite styles to their own needs.

The 20th century brought unprecedented acceleration in the spread of styles, driven by globalization and media. The invention of the cinema turned Hollywood into a fashion capital, with movie stars like Audrey Hepburn and Marilyn Monroe becoming global icons. Their on-screen wardrobes, often designed by top fashion houses, influenced millions worldwide. For instance, the little black dress, popularized by Hepburn in *Breakfast at Tiffany's*, became a staple in wardrobes across continents.

World War II introduced a unique form of style dissemination. Soldiers from various countries stationed abroad brought back clothing and accessories that influenced post-war fashion. American GIs stationed in Europe adopted and modified elements of European style, such as berets and leather jackets. At the same time, the practicality of wartime clothing—like the simple, tailored lines of women's utility suits—laid the groundwork for post-war fashion trends.

The post-war era saw the rise of youth culture as a driving force in fashion's global spread. The 1960s counterculture movements created distinct styles like mod in the UK and hippie in the US, which quickly crossed borders. Music was influential in this process, with rock bands like The Beatles and The Rolling Stones bringing British style to America and beyond. The introduction of denim jeans as a global phenomenon during this time is another example. Originally a durable workwear fabric, denim evolved into a symbol of rebellion and youth, spreading rapidly across continents.

In the late 20th century, fashion became increasingly globalized. Japanese designers like Issey Miyake and Rei Kawakubo introduced avant-garde styles to Western audiences, challenging conventional notions of silhouette and structure. Meanwhile, African and South Asian textiles gained prominence, with patterns like kente cloth and batik appearing on international runways. The blending of global styles into modern fashion reflected a growing appreciation for diverse cultural aesthetics.

Technology revolutionized the spread of style in the 21st century. The internet and social media turned fashion into a borderless industry. Influencers on platforms like Instagram and TikTok now dictate trends to audiences worldwide, often bypassing traditional fashion gatekeepers. Online shopping platforms allow consumers to purchase styles from any corner of the globe with a click, erasing regional limitations.

The spread of style continues to evolve. As cultures interact and technologies advance, fashion remains a fluid, ever-changing reflection of human connection and creativity.

Why Fashion is Cyclical

Fashion operates in cycles, a phenomenon deeply rooted in human behavior, societal dynamics, and technological advancements. The return of trends over decades or centuries isn't random; it's the result of interconnected factors that influence what we wear and why we wear it. From nostalgia and cultural shifts to economic patterns and the human need for novelty, fashion's cyclical nature reveals much about society.

One reason fashion is cyclical is nostalgia. Humans often romanticize the past, and this nostalgia influences clothing preferences. Designers frequently revisit earlier eras, reinterpreting iconic styles for modern audiences. The 1970s resurgence in the late 1990s and early 2000s, with flared jeans, bohemian prints, and platform shoes, wasn't accidental. It reflected a longing for the perceived freedom and individuality of the hippie movement, adapted for a generation craving self-expression during a time of growing globalization.

Technological advancements also drive fashion cycles. New technologies often make older styles easier to produce or more accessible, leading to their revival. For example, in the 1980s, neon colors became popular due to advancements in dyeing processes that made bright, long-lasting pigments feasible. When these neon styles returned in the 2010s, they were bolstered by innovations in synthetic fabrics and a renewed focus on bold, statement-making fashion.

The influence of economic cycles on fashion cannot be understated. During periods of economic hardship, simpler, more practical styles dominate. For instance, the Great Depression of the 1930s saw the rise of modest, utility-focused clothing, with fabrics and cuts designed for longevity. However, as economies recover, fashion often shifts toward extravagance and experimentation. This was evident in the post-World War II era, when Christian Dior introduced his "New Look" in 1947, featuring full skirts and luxurious fabrics that symbolized a return to prosperity. The cyclical pattern of austerity followed by opulence is a recurring theme in fashion history.

Cultural shifts further contribute to fashion's cyclical nature. As societies evolve, they frequently reject the norms of the previous generation, only to rediscover and reinterpret them later. The minimalist aesthetic of the 1990s, characterized by simple silhouettes and neutral tones, was a direct response to the bold, excessive styles of the 1980s. However, as the cultural pendulum swung back, maximalism emerged once again in the 2010s, with bright colors, patterns, and layered textures making a comeback.

Fashion cycles are also influenced by the concept of exclusivity. Trends begin in niche groups or among the elite and eventually trickle down to the masses. Once a style becomes widely adopted, it often loses its appeal to the original trendsetters, who then move on to something new. This phenomenon, known as the "trickle-down effect," ensures the constant turnover of styles. For example, punk fashion, with its torn clothing, safety pins, and combat boots, began as an anti-establishment statement in the 1970s but was commodified and mainstreamed by the 1980s, prompting subcultures to seek new ways to distinguish themselves.

Simultaneously, the "bubble-up effect" describes how styles originating in marginalized or grassroots communities influence mainstream fashion. Streetwear, once associated with urban subcultures, became a global trend in the 2000s, with brands like Supreme and Off-White leading the charge. The cyclical reappropriation of streetwear from niche to mainstream to niche again highlights how cultural dynamics fuel fashion's repetitive nature.

The psychology of novelty has been critical in fashion cycles. Humans are drawn to what feels fresh and exciting, but overexposure to any trend eventually leads to fatigue. This cycle of attraction and rejection ensures that styles constantly rotate. Take the example of skinny jeans: after dominating fashion for over a decade, they began to decline in popularity in the late 2010s, replaced by looser fits and vintage-inspired silhouettes. However, skinny jeans are unlikely to disappear entirely; they may return in a new form, appealing to a future generation seeking something "retro."

Another factor in fashion's cyclical nature is the reinterpretation of historical themes. Designers often find inspiration in the past but adapt it to contemporary sensibilities. The flapper dresses of the 1920s, with their loose silhouettes and shimmering embellishments, experienced a revival in the 1960s and again in the 2010s. Each iteration maintained the essence of the original style but incorporated modern materials and cultural references, making it relevant for new audiences.

Globalization has accelerated fashion cycles, as trends can now spread across the world instantly. Social media platforms like Instagram and TikTok allow styles to emerge, peak, and decline at unprecedented speeds. This rapid turnover often leads to micro-trends, where specific elements of older styles resurface for brief periods before being replaced. For example, the resurgence of 1990s-inspired chokers in the mid-2010s was a fleeting trend, lasting only a few years before fading again.

Economic and environmental sustainability concerns have also shaped recent fashion cycles. The backlash against fast fashion has led to a resurgence of timeless styles, as consumers seek clothing that transcends fleeting trends. Vintage fashion has gained popularity as people turn to thrift stores and secondhand markets, both to reduce waste and to embrace styles from the past. This renewed interest in sustainability has reintroduced designs from decades ago into mainstream fashion, blurring the lines between old and new.

Cultural nostalgia often ties fashion cycles to broader media influences. Movies, television, and music can reignite interest in specific periods, bringing their styles back into the spotlight. For instance, the popularity of the 1980s-set television series *Stranger Things* in the late 2010s coincided with a revival of 1980s fashion, from high-waisted jeans to bold neon colors. Similarly, the 2000s resurgence in the 2020s—dubbed "Y2K fashion"—has been fueled by nostalgia for early internet culture and millennial childhoods.

Even items as personal as men's and women's underwear go through cycles of change influenced by culture, technology, and fashion trends. For example, men's undergarments have shifted from loose-fitting linen breeches in ancient times to snug briefs in the 20th century and back to relaxed boxers, then to hybrid boxer-briefs and more form-fitting brief styles today, reflecting preferences for comfort, utility, and style. Similarly, women's underwear has evolved from restrictive corsetry and bloomers to the minimalist thongs of the 1990s and now to the higher-waisted, full-coverage styles inspired by vintage trends.

These cycles often align with broader societal changes. The 1920s brought lighter, practical undergarments as women embraced freedom of movement, while the 1950s reintroduced structured lingerie like girdles to create the hourglass figure popularized by Dior's New Look. The 21st century sees increasing emphasis on comfort and sustainability, with breathable fabrics and gender-neutral designs gaining traction.

Even within periods of utility, innovation thrives—fabrics like microfiber and modal offer both comfort and performance. Trends in underwear not only mirror shifts in aesthetics but also adapt to changing attitudes about body image, gender roles, and self-expression, making them a small yet powerful reflection of larger cultural dynamics.

Fashion cycles are not only dictated by designers and media but also by consumer demand. The democratization of fashion, particularly through online platforms, allows individuals to influence trends in ways that were impossible before. As consumers mix and match styles from different decades, they create hybrid looks that often lead to the resurgence of forgotten trends. For example, the "cottagecore" aesthetic, which gained traction during the COVID-19 pandemic, drew from Victorian and Edwardian influences, reinterpreted for a modern context.

The cyclical nature of fashion is also tied to generational dynamics. As younger generations come of age, they often reject the styles of their parents, only to rediscover and adopt them later as a form of retro chic. This generational rejection and rediscovery keep older trends in circulation. For example, bell-bottoms, once dismissed as relics of the 1970s, returned in the 1990s and again in the 2020s, each time updated with contemporary details.

Ultimately, fashion cycles persist because they balance familiarity with innovation. The return of past styles provides a sense of continuity and connection to history, while modern reinterpretations keep fashion fresh and relevant. This ensures that even as trends come and go, fashion remains an ever-evolving reflection of humanity.

The Philosophy of Fashion

Fashion, at its core, is a philosophical expression of humanity's relationship with self, society, and the environment. It is more than clothing; it is a complex interplay of identity, meaning, and intention. The philosophy of fashion explores why we wear what we wear and how those choices resonate with deeper existential questions about individuality, community, and values.

One of the foundational aspects of fashion's philosophy is its ability to mediate between the individual and the collective. Clothing serves as both a personal statement and a reflection of societal norms. Philosophers such as Georg Simmel have argued that fashion exists in a tension between the desire to fit in and the desire to stand out. This duality is evident in how trends emerge: individuals adopt popular styles to signal belonging but often modify them to assert uniqueness. A brightly colored scarf paired with a uniform outfit, for example, can convey both conformity and individuality.

Fashion's philosophical significance also lies in its temporality. Unlike art or architecture, fashion is inherently transient, tied to seasons and shifting trends. This ephemerality raises questions about permanence and value. Why do we invest emotionally and financially in garments that will inevitably fall out of style? The answer often lies in fashion's role as a reflection of the moment. A dress might be fleeting, but its connection to a particular cultural, political, or personal experience imbues it with meaning. For instance, the miniskirt of the 1960s wasn't just a garment; it was a statement of liberation and rebellion against conservative values.

The materiality of fashion carries its own philosophical weight. What we choose to wear is shaped by the textures, colors, and structures of fabric, which evoke sensory and emotional responses. Wool, for example, suggests warmth and comfort, while silk evokes luxury and delicacy. These material properties are not neutral; they are imbued with cultural and historical significance. Leather, once a practical material for protective garments, has evolved into a symbol of toughness and rebellion in modern fashion, as seen in the iconic leather jacket.

The ethics of fashion form another pillar of its philosophy. Choices about what to wear are not merely aesthetic but moral decisions, particularly in an age of environmental awareness and globalization. The fast-fashion industry, with its reliance on cheap labor and mass production, raises questions about exploitation and sustainability. Philosophically, wearing a garment made under unethical conditions implicates the wearer in systems of inequality. This awareness has spurred movements toward ethical fashion, where consumers prioritize slow, sustainable, and locally sourced clothing.

Fashion is also a form of communication, a nonverbal language through which individuals express their identity, beliefs, and affiliations. Philosopher Roland Barthes explored this idea in *The Fashion System*, describing how garments function as symbols that carry cultural codes. For instance, a tailored suit signifies professionalism and authority in many contexts, while a hoodie might convey casualness or rebellion, depending on its wearer and setting. These codes, however, are not static; they evolve as society's values shift, revealing the fluidity of fashion as a language.

The philosophical question of freedom is deeply tied to fashion. What does it mean to have the freedom to choose what to wear? In many societies, clothing is regulated by laws, traditions, or social expectations, limiting personal expression. Historical examples abound: sumptuary laws in medieval Europe restricted certain fabrics and colors to the elite, while Victorian dress codes dictated women's modesty through restrictive corsets and long skirts. Even today, dress codes in schools, workplaces, and religious institutions often impose limits on what individuals can wear, sparking debates about autonomy and self-expression.

Cultural appropriation is another area where fashion intersects with philosophy. The borrowing of styles, patterns, or garments from marginalized cultures by dominant groups raises ethical and philosophical questions about ownership, respect, and context. For example, wearing a Native American headdress as a festival accessory strips the garment of its spiritual and ceremonial significance. This misuse highlights the tension between fashion's ability to transcend cultural boundaries and its potential to reinforce power imbalances.

Fashion's relationship with beauty offers rich philosophical terrain. While the concept of beauty is subjective, fashion often dictates what is considered beautiful at a given time. This dynamic can be seen in shifting beauty standards: the full-figured silhouettes of the Renaissance, the androgynous flapper style of the 1920s, and the slim, athletic look of the 21st century. These standards, perpetuated by fashion media and advertising, shape how individuals view their bodies and, by extension, their self-worth. Philosophically, this raises questions about authenticity and the extent to which our choices are influenced by external pressures rather than personal preferences.

Fashion's capacity to disrupt norms is another key element of its philosophy. Avant-garde designers challenge traditional notions of functionality and aesthetics, creating garments that question the boundaries of clothing and art. Rei Kawakubo's work with Comme des Garçons, for instance, has defied conventional ideas of symmetry and wearability, forcing observers to reconsider what constitutes fashion. These disruptions are not just artistic experiments; they are philosophical inquiries into the nature of clothing and its purpose.

Fashion's connection to memory and identity also deserves attention. Garments often carry personal and collective memories, acting as physical artifacts of experiences. A wedding dress, for instance, encapsulates a deeply personal moment, while military uniforms evoke shared histories of sacrifice and service. This ability of clothing to hold and transmit memory ties it to the broader philosophical question of how material objects shape human experience.

The role of fashion in power dynamics cannot be ignored. Clothing has long been used to assert dominance or challenge authority. The suffragettes of the early 20th century deliberately wore feminine yet practical clothing, such as tailored skirts and blouses, to subvert expectations and signal their seriousness as political agents. Similarly, the zoot suit, popular among Mexican-American youth in the 1940s, became a symbol of resistance against cultural assimilation, sparking controversy and even riots.

Fashion also intersects with the philosophy of time. It reflects the present, recalls the past, and anticipates the future. Designers often draw inspiration from historical periods while innovating with modern materials and techniques. The result is a dialogue between eras, where clothing acts as a bridge connecting different points in time. A vintage-inspired dress made from recycled materials, for instance, combines nostalgia with forward-thinking sustainability, encapsulating fashion's ability to traverse temporal boundaries.

The digital age has introduced new philosophical questions about fashion. Virtual clothing, wearable technology, and augmented reality garments challenge the traditional understanding of what clothing is and how it functions. Can a digital dress worn on Instagram have the same meaning or value as a physical one? These innovations force us to reconsider the relationship between fashion and materiality, expanding the possibilities for self-expression while raising concerns about authenticity and permanence.

Ultimately, the philosophy of fashion explores the deep connections between clothing and the human condition. It is not just about what we wear but about why we wear it, how it shapes our interactions, and what it reveals about our place in the world. Each choice we make—whether deliberate or unconscious—contributes to a broader narrative of meaning and identity, woven into the fabric of everyday life.

CHAPTER 2: FASHION IN ANTIQUITY

Egyptian Elegance

Ancient Egypt was a civilization deeply connected to its environment, and its clothing reflected this relationship. With its intense desert heat, the choice of materials, styles, and colors all served both practical and symbolic purposes. Egyptian fashion wasn't just about protection from the elements; it was a system of social, spiritual, and political expression. Every garment, accessory, and adornment carried meaning, speaking volumes about the wearer's role and identity within the society.

The foundation of Egyptian clothing was linen. This lightweight fabric, made from the fibers of the flax plant, was ideal for the hot climate. Flax was grown along the Nile River, where the fertile soil and plentiful water ensured abundant crops. After harvesting, flax stalks were soaked and beaten to release the fibers, which were then spun into thread. Egyptian linen was renowned for its quality. The finest varieties, called *byssus*, were almost transparent and reserved for the elite. Linen's natural whiteness was highly valued, symbolizing purity and sacredness. Unlike other ancient civilizations that used wool or animal hides extensively, Egyptians avoided these materials in favor of linen, associating wool with impurity and limiting its use to certain religious rituals.

Clothing styles in Egypt were simple but elegant. For much of the Old and Middle Kingdom periods, men typically wore a *shendyt*, a kilt-like garment made from a rectangular piece of linen wrapped around the waist and secured with a belt. The length of the *shendyt* varied over time. Early examples were short, reaching mid-thigh, but by the New Kingdom, they often extended to the knees or even the ankles. Pleating, a hallmark of Egyptian textiles, added texture and sophistication. These pleats weren't merely decorative—they required skillful craftsmanship, demonstrating the artistry of Egyptian weavers.

Women's garments were equally refined. The most common attire was the *kalasiris*, a sheath dress that fit snugly around the body and extended from the chest or shoulders to the ankles. Early depictions show the dress as sleeveless, while later versions incorporated wide straps or even sleeves. The *kalasiris* was often paired with an over-garment, such as a shawl or cape, which added layers of complexity to the outfit. Elite women adorned their *kalasiris* with intricate beading or embroidery, though the base material remained linen. The combination of simplicity in design and luxurious embellishments made Egyptian clothing timelessly elegant.

Color was another significant aspect of Egyptian fashion. While the natural whiteness of linen dominated, colored garments were also popular among the wealthy. Dyes made from plants, minerals, and insects created vibrant hues. Indigo and woad produced blues, while madder root yielded reds. Yellow, derived from saffron or pomegranate rind, and green from malachite were also used. These dyes were expensive, labor-intensive to produce, and thus became markers of status. In contrast, the lower classes typically wore undyed garments.

Jewelry was indispensable in Egyptian fashion, serving both decorative and symbolic purposes. Necklaces, bracelets, rings, and anklets adorned nearly everyone, regardless of class, but the materials and designs varied widely. Gold, sourced from mines in Nubia, was the most prized material and symbolized divine power. Semi-precious stones such as turquoise, carnelian, and lapis lazuli added vibrant color and spiritual significance to the pieces. The *wesekh* collar, a broad, flat necklace that covered the shoulders and upper chest, was an iconic element of Egyptian fashion. Often made of gold and inlaid with stones, the *wesekh* symbolized protection and wealth. Amulets were also common, worn as pendants or sewn into clothing to invoke the protection of gods or to represent specific virtues. The Eye of Horus, scarabs, and ankhs were among the most popular motifs.

Hairstyles and headgear further elevated Egyptian elegance. Men and women alike often shaved their heads, particularly among the upper classes, to maintain hygiene in the hot climate. Wigs made from human hair or plant fibers were worn on special occasions, styled into elaborate shapes and often adorned with gold bands or floral decorations. These wigs were not merely practical; they were status symbols, indicating wealth and refinement. Pharaohs wore the iconic *nemes* headdress, a striped cloth draped over the head and shoulders, symbolizing their divine authority. Queens and priestesses often wore diadems or crowns embellished with motifs like the vulture or cobra, representing protection and royalty.

Footwear in ancient Egypt was minimal. Most people went barefoot, but sandals made of papyrus or leather were common among the upper classes. These sandals were simple in design, but elite individuals often had pairs decorated with gold leaf or intricate patterns. For ceremonial purposes, sandals could be adorned with images of conquered enemies, a symbolic gesture of dominance and control.

Religious and ceremonial attire demonstrated the intersection of fashion and spirituality in Egypt. Priests wore simple, white linen robes, reflecting their role as intermediaries between the gods and the people. Certain rituals required priests to abstain from wearing wool or leather, which were considered impure. The Pharaoh's ceremonial attire was the most elaborate, designed to emphasize his divine status. The *sed-festival robe*, worn during a jubilee celebrating a Pharaoh's reign, featured pleated linen, gold ornaments, and the *false beard*, a symbolic accessory indicating kingship.

Funerary fashion provides further insights into Egyptian elegance. Mummies were often wrapped in multiple layers of fine linen, a process that required hundreds of yards of fabric. The wealthiest individuals were buried with jewelry, amulets, and even miniature models of their favorite garments. The inclusion of these items reflected the belief that clothing and adornments were as essential in the afterlife as they were in daily life. Golden masks, such as the famous mask of Tutankhamun, were placed over the faces of mummies to signify the individual's divine nature and eternal beauty.

Fashion in Egypt also reflected its interactions with neighboring cultures. During the New Kingdom, trade and conquest brought new materials and styles into Egyptian wardrobes. Nubian gold, Levantine dyes, and Minoan-inspired patterns enriched Egyptian design. The depiction of foreign captives wearing distinctive garments in tomb paintings highlights the Egyptians' awareness of and influence on the clothing traditions of other cultures.

Fashion was also deeply tied to festivals and celebrations. During religious festivals, both men and women wore their finest garments, often adorned with fresh flowers. The use of perfume cones, made from scented fat that slowly melted in the heat, was another unique aspect of Egyptian festival attire. These cones not only added fragrance but also served as a visual display of wealth and festivity.

Children's clothing, or the lack thereof, further illustrates the practicality of Egyptian fashion. Until the age of six or seven, children typically went unclothed, especially in lower-class families. Wealthier families might dress their children in simple linen tunics or adorn them with jewelry, such as bracelets or anklets, to signify their status.

Egyptian fashion was not static. Over thousands of years, styles evolved in response to changes in political power, trade, and cultural influences. For example, during the Amarna period under Akhenaten, a shift toward more naturalistic and flowing clothing styles reflected the radical religious and artistic changes of the time. Women's dresses became more voluminous, and depictions of royal figures included previously unseen elements, such as pleated capes and elaborate sashes.

Through its emphasis on simplicity, sophistication, and symbolism, Egyptian fashion remains one of the most enduring and iconic examples of ancient clothing. It set standards not only for practical wear but also for the integration of artistry, spirituality, and societal structure into every aspect of dress.

Greek Drapery

Ancient Greek fashion was a masterclass in simplicity and elegance. Unlike many cultures that relied on cutting and sewing to create fitted garments, the Greeks perfected the art of draping rectangular pieces of fabric over the body. This approach emphasized form, fluidity, and functionality, resulting in clothing that was both practical and beautiful. Greek drapery wasn't merely about covering the body; it was an expression of identity, a statement of societal values, and an enduring legacy that influenced fashion for centuries.

The cornerstone of Greek clothing was the *chiton*, a rectangular piece of linen or wool fabric. It was folded and wrapped around the body, secured with pins, buttons, or belts. There were two primary types: the *doric chiton* and the *ionic chiton*. The *doric chiton*, a more conservative style, was made from heavier fabric like wool. It featured minimal pleats and was fastened at the shoulders with *fibulae* (decorative pins). This style was practical and reserved, often associated with ideals of modesty and traditional values.

The *ionic chiton* was more elaborate, crafted from lighter fabrics such as linen. It featured abundant pleats and was fastened with multiple pins along the shoulders and arms, creating voluminous, flowing sleeves. This version allowed for greater movement and was often seen as more elegant and sophisticated. Both types of *chitons* could be cinched at the waist with a belt or girdle, which emphasized the natural curves of the body. The Greeks used this simple design to highlight the human form, rather than conceal it, reflecting their admiration for balance and proportion.

The *himation* was another essential element of Greek drapery. It was a larger, heavier rectangular piece of fabric, typically wool, that was draped over the shoulders and wrapped around the body. The *himation* could be worn alone or over a *chiton*, serving as a cloak or a formal outer garment. Its arrangement varied depending on the occasion and the wearer's social status. For instance, philosophers and statesmen often wore the *himation* in a way that left one arm uncovered, allowing for expressive gestures during public speaking. This style became a visual shorthand for intellectual authority.

For more casual wear or colder weather, the *chlamys* was a popular choice, particularly among men. This shorter cloak, fastened with a single pin at the shoulder, was favored by soldiers and travelers for its practicality. Unlike the flowing elegance of the *himation*, the *chlamys* was tightly draped and allowed for ease of movement, making it a functional yet stylish garment.

Women's garments, while similar in construction to men's, often included additional layers and embellishments. The *peplos*, an early form of Greek dress, was a rectangular piece of wool fabric folded down at the top to create a double-layered bodice. It was then secured at the shoulders with pins and cinched at the waist, creating a column-like silhouette. The *peplos* was particularly associated with religious rituals and traditional festivals, as it symbolized ancient customs and feminine virtue.

Colors and patterns were common in Greek drapery, though the palette was often understated. Natural dyes derived from plants and minerals produced earthy tones such as ochre, brown, and pale green. Wealthier Greeks could afford brighter hues, such as deep reds and purples, achieved using more expensive dyes like *Tyrian purple*, extracted from sea snails. Patterns were added through weaving or embroidery, with common motifs including meanders (Greek keys), floral designs, and mythological scenes. These embellishments were not merely decorative; they often carried symbolic meaning, connecting the wearer to cultural ideals, religious beliefs, or personal achievements.

Greek drapery was designed to be adaptable. The same piece of fabric could be styled in multiple ways, making it suitable for a variety of occasions. This versatility extended to gender and age as well. While men's drapery tended to be simpler, women's garments were longer and more layered, reflecting societal roles and expectations. Children often wore smaller versions of adult garments, though they might go unclothed in the warmest months until reaching adolescence.

Accessories further enhanced Greek fashion. *Fibulae*, the pins used to secure garments, ranged from simple bronze fasteners to elaborate designs made of gold or silver, often inlaid with gemstones. Belts or girdles, made of leather or woven fabric, added structure to the loose garments. Footwear, though not always worn, typically consisted of sandals made from leather or woven materials. In more formal settings, men and women might wear *kothornoi*, high-soled sandals that added height and drama to their appearance.

Headgear also had an important role in Greek fashion. Women often wore veils or scarves, such as the *kredemnon*, which could be draped over the head and shoulders. These coverings were both practical, offering protection from the sun, and symbolic, representing modesty and decorum. Men might wear simple caps like the *petasos*, a broad-brimmed hat associated with travelers and farmers. For formal occasions, wreaths made of laurel, olive, or ivy leaves were common, symbolizing victory, honor, or divine favor.

Greek drapery wasn't only about personal expression; it was deeply tied to civic identity and public life. The garments worn during religious ceremonies, festivals, and public gatherings often adhered to specific conventions, reinforcing communal values. For example, during the Panathenaic Festival in Athens, women wove a ceremonial peplos for the statue of Athena, their patron goddess. This act wasn't just a display of skill but a reaffirmation of the city's cultural and spiritual unity.

Gender distinctions in Greek drapery extended to the symbolic use of clothing. Men's garments often left parts of the body exposed, emphasizing physical strength and athleticism, ideals central to Greek masculinity. In contrast, women's clothing was designed to highlight grace and modesty, reflecting societal expectations of femininity. However, these distinctions weren't rigid. In theatrical performances, male actors often donned women's drapery to portray female characters, using layers and props to exaggerate feminine traits for dramatic effect.

Trade and cultural exchange introduced new elements into Greek fashion. Contact with the Persian Empire brought luxurious fabrics like silk and techniques such as pleating, which influenced Greek textile production. Egyptian linen, highly prized for its quality, became a staple material for lightweight summer garments. These interactions enriched Greek drapery, blending local traditions with foreign innovations to create styles that were both distinctive and cosmopolitan.

Greek drapery's influence extended far beyond its own time. During the Roman Empire, Greek styles were adapted into Roman garments such as the *tunic* and *stola*. Later, during the Renaissance, European artists and designers looked to ancient Greek drapery for inspiration, using its flowing lines and harmonious proportions to inform both fashion and art. Even in modern fashion, Greek drapery serves as a reference point, appearing in evening gowns, bridal dresses, and haute couture collections.

At its heart, Greek drapery was a celebration of balance—between simplicity and elegance, utility and beauty. Its enduring appeal lies in its ability to showcase the human form while reflecting the values of the society that created it. Every fold, pleat, and pin told a story, one that continues to resonate across cultures and centuries.

Roman Innovations

Roman fashion was a blend of practicality and status, deeply influenced by the cultures they encountered through conquest and trade. The Romans borrowed heavily from Greek fashion but introduced innovations that reflected their distinct values and social systems. Clothing in Rome was not just about covering the body; it was a tool for communication, conveying rank, citizenship, and moral standing. Each garment, accessory, and material carried specific meanings, creating a sophisticated visual language.

The **tunic** was the most basic and versatile garment in Roman fashion. Men, women, and children wore tunics, though their design and length varied by gender, age, and status. Roman tunics were simple in construction, made from two pieces of rectangular fabric sewn together at the sides, leaving openings for the head and arms. They were typically made from wool or linen, depending on the season, and cinched at the waist with a belt. For men, tunics generally reached the knees, allowing for ease of movement, while women's tunics were longer, reaching the ankles. Citizens and slaves alike wore tunics, but the quality of the fabric and the presence of embellishments distinguished their social positions.

One of Rome's most iconic garments, the **toga**, symbolized Roman citizenship and its accompanying privileges. Reserved exclusively for free Roman men, the toga was a large semicircular piece of woolen fabric draped over the body in an intricate fashion. The process of donning a toga was complex and often required assistance, reflecting its ceremonial and symbolic importance. Togas came in different colors and patterns, each with its own meaning. For example, the **toga praetexta**, bordered with a purple stripe, was worn by senators and magistrates, signifying authority. The **toga candida**, a dazzling white toga treated with chalk, was worn by political candidates to project purity and honesty. Meanwhile, the **toga pulla**, made of dark wool, was worn during periods of mourning, showing the versatility of this garment as a medium of expression.

The Romans introduced **garment layering** to accommodate their expanding empire's diverse climates. While the toga was prominent in public life, cloaks like the **pallium** and **lacerna** offered additional warmth and functionality. The pallium, adapted from the Greek himation, was a rectangular piece of fabric draped over the shoulders. It was lighter than the toga and often used as a more casual alternative. The lacerna, a shorter cloak, came with a hood and was especially practical for soldiers and travelers. These garments showcased the Roman ability to adapt existing designs to meet practical needs.

Women's clothing in Rome also reflected a balance of tradition and innovation. The **stola**, a long dress worn over a tunic, was the traditional attire of married Roman women. It was distinctively Roman, differentiating itself from the simpler Greek chitons. The stola was typically made from wool or linen, though wealthier women opted for silk or dyed fabrics. A decorative border or band, called the **instita**, adorned the stola, signifying modesty and virtue. Women often layered the stola with a **palla**, a rectangular shawl that could be draped over the shoulders or head. The palla added elegance and modesty, aligning with Roman ideals of femininity.

Color and ornamentation were essential in Roman fashion, with dyes and patterns signifying wealth and status. The Romans utilized a wide range of natural dyes, including red from madder, yellow from saffron, and blue from woad. Purple, however, was the most prestigious and expensive dye, derived from the secretions of the Murex sea snail. Known as **Tyrian purple**, this dye was so costly that only the emperor and his family could afford garments dyed entirely in this color. This exclusivity made purple the ultimate status symbol, associating it with imperial authority.

Roman military attire was both functional and symbolic. Soldiers wore tunics under their armor, but these tunics were shorter and often dyed red, a color associated with Mars, the god of war. The **paludamentum**, a red or purple cloak fastened at the shoulder, was worn by generals during military campaigns, signifying leadership and command. Footwear for soldiers was equally innovative. The **caligae**, heavy-duty sandals reinforced with iron nails, provided durability and traction during long marches, showcasing the Roman emphasis on practicality in design.

Footwear in Rome reflected the wearer's social standing and occupation. Sandals, or **soleae**, were common among all classes, but the materials and craftsmanship varied widely. Wealthy Romans wore sandals made from fine leather, often decorated with gold or silver accents. For colder weather, the **calceus**, a closed shoe, was preferred. Patricians distinguished themselves with red or black calcei, while senators wore footwear adorned with crescent-shaped decorations called **lunulae**. These subtle details allowed Romans to visually assert their rank without verbal introductions.

Jewelry and personal adornment were equally significant in Roman fashion, particularly for women. Wealthy women adorned themselves with necklaces, bracelets, rings, and earrings made from gold, silver, and gemstones like emeralds and pearls. The **fibula**, a brooch used to fasten garments, was both practical and decorative, often crafted with intricate designs. Men, too, wore jewelry, though typically in more understated forms, such as rings that doubled as signet seals for stamping documents.

Romans were innovators in textile production, refining techniques for spinning, weaving, and dyeing fabrics. Wool was the most commonly used material, as sheep farming was widespread across the empire. Linen, imported from Egypt, provided a cooler alternative for the warmer months. Silk, introduced through trade with China along the Silk Road, became a coveted luxury item among the elite. Romans were among the first to mix silk with wool to create a hybrid fabric known as **holosericum**, combining the softness of silk with the durability of wool. This innovation not only made silk more accessible but also demonstrated the Roman penchant for practicality.

The care and maintenance of garments were important aspects of Roman life. Clothes were frequently laundered at communal fullonicae, or laundry facilities, where fullers used a mixture of water, clay, and even urine to clean and whiten fabrics. This process highlights the communal nature of Roman society and its reliance on shared resources for everyday needs.

Religious rituals and ceremonies heavily influenced Roman fashion. Priests and priestesses wore specific garments to reflect their roles. The **flamines**, priests dedicated to individual deities, wore distinctive caps called **apices** and draped themselves in white robes to symbolize purity. The **vestal virgins**, priestesses of Vesta, wore a unique headdress called the **infula**, a woolen band that encircled their heads, signifying their sacred duty.

Roman fashion was deeply connected to the legal and moral codes of the time. Sumptuary laws regulated who could wear certain colors, fabrics, and accessories, ensuring that clothing reflected societal hierarchies. For example, slaves and freedmen were prohibited from wearing the toga, marking their lower status. Freedmen, however, often wore a **pileus**, a felt cap symbolizing their emancipation, making it a powerful emblem of their newfound freedom.

The Romans also influenced fashion through their widespread trade networks. Imported textiles, such as Egyptian linen, Indian cotton, and Chinese silk, introduced new materials and designs to Roman wardrobes. These goods were often reinterpreted to suit Roman tastes, blending foreign influences with local traditions. The integration of diverse styles demonstrates the cosmopolitan nature of Roman fashion and its ability to adapt and innovate.

Hairstyles were another area where the Romans showcased creativity and innovation. Women's hairstyles became increasingly elaborate over time, with intricate braids, curls, and adornments like pins and combs. During the Flavian dynasty, towering, curled hairstyles became popular among elite women, requiring hours of labor by skilled hairdressers. Men's hairstyles, though simpler, reflected changing trends, from the clean-shaven look of early Rome to the bearded style popularized by Emperor Hadrian.

Roman innovations in fashion extended beyond clothing and accessories to societal norms. Clothing served as a tool for defining citizenship, gender roles, and moral values, illustrating the Romans' ability to use fashion as both a practical necessity and a means of cultural expression. Their contributions to textile production, garment design, and symbolic dress left a lasting legacy, influencing the development of fashion in the centuries that followed.

Persian and Eastern Influences

Persian fashion was an elegant combination of practicality, luxury, and symbolism. As one of the most influential empires of antiquity, Persia connected the East and West, introducing sophisticated textile techniques, intricate patterns, and innovative garments that spread far beyond its borders. Persian clothing was deeply tied to the empire's geography, culture, and social structure, and its influence can be traced in the fashion of Greece, Rome, and even later medieval Europe.

One of the most notable Persian contributions to fashion was the introduction of tailored garments. While draped clothing dominated the Mediterranean, Persian clothing emphasized fitted designs. The Persians were among the first to develop and popularize trousers. These garments, called *sharovary*, were practical for horseback riding, a necessity for the nomadic and later imperial lifestyles of the Persian people. Made from durable wool or fine silk for the elite, these trousers symbolized both functionality and innovation. They were adopted by neighboring cultures, including the Greeks, who initially saw them as foreign but gradually appreciated their practicality for soldiers and travelers.

The **kandys**, a long coat with wide sleeves, was another iconic Persian garment. Worn by both men and women, it was often crafted from wool, leather, or luxurious fabrics like silk. The kandys could be draped over the shoulders or worn with the arms in the sleeves, making it versatile for different climates and occasions. Its design influenced the *chlamys* of the Greeks and later the cloaks of Roman nobility. The kandys wasn't just a coat; it was a symbol of Persian refinement, particularly when embellished with embroidery or dyed in vibrant colors.

Color and dyeing techniques in Persia set new standards for luxury. Persian artisans mastered the use of indigo for deep blues, madder for rich reds, and saffron for golden yellows. Tyrian purple, although more associated with Phoenicians, was highly prized in Persia as well. These colors weren't just decorative—they signified status. Persian nobility often wore robes in striking hues, adorned with patterns of flora, fauna, and mythical creatures. These motifs weren't arbitrary; they reflected Zoroastrian beliefs and cosmological themes, linking clothing to religion and philosophy.

The Achaemenid Empire (550–330 BCE) was a turning point for Persian fashion. Under the rule of Cyrus the Great and later Darius I, Persia became a melting pot of cultures, incorporating styles from conquered territories like Babylon, Egypt, and India. This cultural exchange enriched Persian clothing, resulting in garments that combined local traditions with imperial grandeur. For instance, the **Elamite influence** introduced the use of pleated skirts and layered garments into Persian wardrobes, while Egyptian linen became a sought-after material for undergarments and summer wear.

Silk, introduced through trade with China, revolutionized Persian textiles. While silk production wasn't native to Persia during the Achaemenid period, Persian traders were influential in its distribution. They combined silk with local materials like wool to create fabrics that were lightweight yet warm, ideal for the empire's diverse climates. The use of silk wasn't limited to the elite; its availability through trade meant that even the middle class could access silk blends, albeit less ornate than those worn by nobility.

Embroidery and patterning were hallmarks of Persian fashion. Persian artisans excelled in creating intricate designs using gold and silver threads, adding a sense of opulence to everyday garments. Patterns often featured repeating geometric shapes, stylized flowers, or mythical creatures like griffins and winged bulls. These designs served not only as decoration but also as symbols of power and divine protection. The techniques developed by Persian weavers influenced the production of textiles across the ancient world, particularly in the Byzantine and later Islamic empires.

Accessories were another key element of Persian fashion. Belts made of leather or embroidered fabric were used to cinch tunics and robes at the waist, creating a tailored silhouette. Jewelry was abundant, with gold and semi-precious stones like carnelian, turquoise, and lapis lazuli adorning necklaces, bracelets, and earrings. Persian crowns, or *diadems*, were highly intricate, often decorated with gemstones and symbolic motifs like the lotus flower, which represented immortality.

Footwear in Persia was practical but often elaborate. Soft leather boots and sandals were common, but the wealthiest individuals wore shoes embroidered with gold thread or inlaid with precious stones. These shoes were not meant for everyday use but were reserved for ceremonial occasions, where every detail of the attire was designed to project power and wealth.

Headgear in Persian fashion was equally significant. The **tiara**, a tall, conical hat, was worn by Persian kings and high-ranking officials, symbolizing their authority. Common people often wore simple cloth headwraps or felt caps to protect against the sun. Women, particularly in the later Sassanian period (224–651 CE), began wearing veils as part of their public attire, a practice that reflected both modesty and social status. The use of veils in Persia influenced similar customs in neighboring regions and later Islamic cultures.

Persian fashion also reflected its military heritage. Soldiers wore functional yet visually striking uniforms that incorporated tunics, trousers, and cloaks. Armor was often made of scale or chainmail, worn over padded tunics. High-ranking officers and commanders distinguished themselves with richly dyed garments and gold-embellished belts or helmets. Military attire wasn't just about protection; it was a statement of the empire's power and technological prowess.

The Persian court set the standard for luxury, and foreign emissaries often remarked on its splendor. At ceremonial gatherings, the king and his courtiers donned robes made of the finest fabrics, embroidered with gold and silver threads. The king's attire included the **khaftan**, a long robe worn over a tunic, often lined with fur or trimmed with gold. The khaftan's design influenced later Islamic and Ottoman fashion, demonstrating Persia's enduring impact on clothing styles.

Trade was a critical avenue for spreading Persian fashion. The Persian Empire's vast network of roads, including the Royal Road, facilitated the exchange of goods and ideas across regions. Persian textiles, particularly those made from silk and fine wool, were highly sought after in Greece, Egypt, and Rome. Greek pottery and sculptures often depict figures wearing Persian-inspired garments, such as fitted trousers and elaborately patterned cloaks. This blending of styles highlights how deeply Persian fashion influenced its neighbors.

Persian fashion evolved further during the Sassanian Empire, known for its opulent textiles and lavish court attire. Sassanian garments were characterized by bold patterns, including roundels and medallions filled with imagery of animals, plants, and mythical figures. These designs were often woven directly into the fabric using advanced techniques like **brocade weaving**, which required exceptional skill. Sassanian textiles became prized exports, influencing Byzantine fashion and later medieval European clothing.

Religious practices also shaped Persian attire. Zoroastrian priests wore white robes to symbolize purity, often paired with a **padan**, a cloth used to cover the mouth during rituals to prevent pollution of the sacred fire. Clothing for religious ceremonies often included specific colors and motifs that aligned with Zoroastrian cosmology, such as the sun or stars, emphasizing the connection between earthly attire and spiritual beliefs.

Persian women's fashion blended elegance with modesty. Long tunics and robes were common, often paired with belts or sashes to create a defined silhouette. Fabrics ranged from simple wools to luxurious silks, depending on the wearer's status. Embroidered veils or shawls added a layer of sophistication, reflecting the wearer's wealth and social position. Jewelry, particularly earrings and bracelets, was an essential part of women's attire, highlighting their role within the family and society.

The influence of Persian fashion persisted long after the empire's decline. Byzantine clothing, with its richly patterned textiles and emphasis on luxurious materials, borrowed heavily from Sassanian designs. Even in modern times, elements of Persian attire, such as embroidered fabrics and flowing robes, continue to inspire designers worldwide.

CHAPTER 3: MEDIEVAL MODES

The Influence of the Church

During the medieval period, the Church dominated nearly every aspect of life, including fashion. Its teachings and authority shaped how people dressed, directly and indirectly. From strict rules on modesty to the symbolic clothing worn by clergy, the Church didn't just reflect the culture of the time; it dictated it. Clothing became a visual marker of piety, morality, and social status, often linked to religious ideals.

Modesty was one of the primary values the Church imposed on fashion. Both men and women were expected to dress in a way that minimized the exposure of the body. This expectation stemmed from the Church's teachings, which associated modest clothing with moral integrity. Necklines were high, sleeves were long, and hemlines extended to the ground. For women, hair was often covered with veils, hoods, or wimples to maintain modesty, reflecting Biblical injunctions about covering one's head. Even in warmer climates, the pressure to conform to these standards of modesty outweighed practical considerations.

Religious symbolism heavily influenced the design and color of clothing. Certain colors, like white, represented purity and were often reserved for special occasions such as baptisms or weddings. Blue, associated with the Virgin Mary, was another popular color, particularly for women's garments. Wealthier individuals who could afford dyes often chose blue to signal both piety and status. On the other hand, black became associated with solemnity and mourning, reflecting its use by the clergy.

The Church imposed sumptuary laws to maintain a clear distinction between social classes and enforce moral behavior. These laws regulated what people could wear based on their rank and income. For example, silk and gold-threaded fabrics were restricted to the upper classes, and only nobility could wear certain furs like ermine. These rules had a moral underpinning, as the Church condemned excessive displays of wealth, labeling them as sinful vanity. However, these laws often created tension, as wealthy merchants sought to emulate the nobility by adopting similar styles, leading to frequent updates and stricter enforcement.

Clergy garments set the standard for much of medieval fashion. The Church required its members to wear clothing that reflected their roles and reinforced their authority. The basic robe, or *cappa*, was the foundation of clerical attire. Priests wore long, loose-fitting garments made from plain materials, emphasizing humility and rejecting worldly excess. Bishops and other high-ranking officials, however, wore more elaborate robes, often adorned with gold embroidery and intricate designs.

These garments were not about personal vanity but about reflecting the splendor of God and the Church.

One of the most distinctive pieces of clerical attire was the *chasuble*, worn during the Mass. This outer garment, often richly decorated with crosses, Biblical scenes, or geometric patterns, symbolized the role of the priest as a mediator between God and the congregation. The *stole*, a long scarf-like piece draped around the neck, further distinguished the clergy. Its use and design varied based on rank and occasion, but it always carried deep religious symbolism.

Monastic orders adopted simpler clothing to reflect their vows of poverty and humility. Monks wore robes made from coarse wool, often in shades of brown, black, or gray. The designs were intentionally unadorned, with no embroidery or embellishments. The famous *habit* of the Franciscans, for instance, consisted of a plain brown robe tied at the waist with a rope belt, symbolizing simplicity and devotion. Nuns' habits followed similar principles, often incorporating veils to maintain modesty and humility.

Pilgrimages and religious ceremonies also influenced lay fashion. Pilgrims traveling to holy sites often wore distinctive garments, such as cloaks emblazoned with symbols of their destinations. For example, a scallop shell sewn onto a cloak or hat indicated a pilgrimage to Santiago de Compostela. These items identified the wearer as a pilgrim and sometimes granted them protection or privileges along their journey.

Festive and religious occasions brought temporary relaxation of strict fashion norms. During Easter or Christmas celebrations, people wore their finest clothing, often borrowing elements of clerical attire in their designs. Rich fabrics, such as velvet and brocade, became more common for feast days, and individuals adorned themselves with jewelry and accessories to honor the occasion. These moments of splendor, however, were always contextualized within the Church's teachings about moderation and humility.

The Church's influence extended to how clothing was made and sold. Many textile guilds operated under the patronage of local churches, and their activities were regulated by religious principles. Guild members often dedicated their work to saints, with specific saints becoming patrons of weavers, dyers, and tailors. Religious festivals frequently involved the blessing of textiles and tools, further reinforcing the connection between fashion and faith.

Art and literature of the medieval period often depicted Biblical figures wearing medieval clothing styles, which reflected the Church's role in shaping contemporary fashion. Paintings of saints, for example, showed them in modest robes that mirrored the everyday garments of the time but imbued them with spiritual significance. This artistic choice not only reinforced the Church's teachings about humility but also provided a visual model for pious attire.

Fashion was also used to enforce social discipline and punishment within the Church's framework. Penitents, for instance, were often required to wear special garments as a sign of repentance. These could include sackcloth, a coarse fabric associated with mourning and penance. Public sinners might be required to don garments marked with a cross or other symbols, visually identifying their status to the community. This practice highlighted the Church's ability to control not only spiritual but also social aspects of life.

Despite its focus on modesty and simplicity, the Church occasionally set fashion trends among the laity, particularly through the visibility of high-ranking clergy. The elaborate robes and jeweled accessories of bishops and cardinals inspired similar designs in court fashion. The pointed shoes, or *poulaine*, popular among European nobility in the 14th century, were originally influenced by clerical footwear. This demonstrates how even an institution advocating humility could inadvertently spark trends.

Religious orders also influenced textile innovations. Monasteries often managed large-scale sheep farming operations, producing high-quality wool for both clerical and lay use. They experimented with dyeing techniques and weaving patterns, many of which became standard practices in medieval Europe. The Cistercian order, known for its emphasis on labor, contributed to the widespread availability of durable, high-quality woolen fabrics.

The rise of Gothic architecture paralleled changes in clerical attire, as both reflected the Church's evolving aesthetics. Clerical garments became more voluminous, with long, flowing sleeves and intricate embroidery mirroring the grandeur of Gothic cathedrals. Liturgical vestments incorporated gold thread and gemstones, symbolizing the light of God. These garments not only served practical purposes during religious ceremonies but also acted as visual extensions of the Church's spiritual and cultural authority.

Even in death, the Church influenced fashion. Burial garments often followed religious guidelines, with the deceased dressed in simple shrouds or habits, particularly if they were members of monastic orders. Wealthier individuals sometimes chose to be buried in garments resembling clerical robes, emphasizing their piety and connection to the Church. Tomb effigies frequently depicted individuals wearing clothing that highlighted their social and religious roles, further immortalizing the Church's impact on medieval fashion.

The Church's dominance over medieval fashion was not without its critics. As wealthier clergy adopted more luxurious attire, some reform movements within the Church called for a return to simplicity, condemning the opulence as hypocritical. These tensions reflected broader societal debates about the balance between spiritual devotion and worldly excess.

Overall, the Church not only influenced personal appearance but also reinforced societal hierarchies, values, and behaviors. Its reach extended from the intricate embroidery of a bishop's robe to the coarse wool of a penitent's sackcloth, leaving an indelible mark on the fashion of the medieval world.

Sumptuary Laws and Class Distinction

Sumptuary laws were one of the most direct ways medieval authorities, including both the Church and secular rulers, controlled fashion. These laws were designed to maintain the social hierarchy by dictating who could wear what based on their class, income, or occupation. Fashion became a clear visual marker of status, and these laws ensured that the distinctions between the wealthy and the common folk were always visible.

The origins of sumptuary laws in medieval Europe can be traced back to concerns about moral behavior and economic stability. The Church viewed excessive spending on clothing as a sign of vanity and warned against it in sermons. Meanwhile, monarchs and nobles feared that the rising merchant class, with its newfound wealth, would blur the lines between traditional social ranks. By restricting access to luxurious materials and embellishments, the elite preserved their exclusive status.

One of the most common targets of sumptuary laws was the use of **luxurious fabrics** like silk, velvet, and brocade. Silk, imported from Asia via trade routes, was one of the most coveted materials. Laws in England during the 14th century, such as the Sumptuary Statutes of Edward III, forbade anyone below the rank of knight from wearing silk. Similarly, velvet, a fabric associated with opulence due to its soft texture and complex weaving process, was restricted to the upper classes. These fabrics symbolized wealth and privilege, and their scarcity made them potent status markers.

Colors were another element strictly regulated by sumptuary laws. Certain dyes, particularly **Tyrian purple**, were prohibitively expensive due to their labor-intensive production. In medieval England, only royalty and the highest-ranking nobility were allowed to wear this shade. Red, derived from cochineal or madder, was also limited to specific ranks, as its vibrant hue indicated wealth. Lower classes were often restricted to wearing earthy tones like brown and gray, which were easier and cheaper to produce using local plants and minerals.

Fur, particularly from animals like ermine, sable, and mink, was a key indicator of class distinction. In France, the 13th-century *Grand Ordonnance* explicitly forbade peasants and merchants from wearing garments trimmed with ermine or other expensive furs. Only the nobility could afford these luxurious additions, and their use in collars, sleeves, and linings became a visual shorthand for wealth and rank. Lower-ranking individuals were limited to cheaper furs like rabbit or sheepskin, which offered practicality without challenging the status quo.

Accessories and embellishments were also subject to regulation. In England, laws restricted the use of gold, silver, and precious stones in clothing to the highest social tiers. Buttons, though ubiquitous today, were once luxury items made from precious metals or gemstones, and their use was similarly controlled. Decorative embroidery, particularly with gold or silk thread, was another restricted feature. Commoners were allowed only plain clothing, while the nobility could flaunt elaborate designs on their tunics, gowns, and mantles.

Sumptuary laws weren't limited to materials and colors—they also addressed the cut and length of garments. Long robes with trailing sleeves, known as **cotehardies**, became a symbol of wealth because they wasted fabric. These garments were often outlawed for lower classes, who were required to wear simpler, more practical designs. In Florence, a 14th-century law prohibited women of the merchant class from wearing gowns with trains longer than two feet, reserving such extravagance for the aristocracy.

The enforcement of sumptuary laws was often uneven and challenging. Wealthy merchants and other rising classes frequently ignored these restrictions, using their resources to emulate the nobility. This led to periodic revisions and stricter penalties. In some cases, violators were fined or had their illegal garments confiscated. However, the persistence of such transgressions highlights the desire of lower classes to assert their success and challenge rigid social structures.

Marriage and wedding attire were also subject to sumptuary laws, as these events provided opportunities for individuals to showcase their wealth. In 14th-century Venice, brides from non-noble families were forbidden from wearing jewels or dresses trimmed with pearls. This ensured that the nobility maintained their unique status even during significant public celebrations. These restrictions extended to dowries, limiting the value of clothing and accessories included as part of marriage negotiations.

Sumptuary laws were not just about preserving class distinctions; they also reflected economic concerns. Rulers sought to prevent excessive spending on imported luxury goods, which could drain local economies. By encouraging the use of locally produced materials like wool and linen, these laws supported domestic industries. For instance, in England, the government promoted the use of woolen garments, aligning with the country's significant wool trade. The restrictions on foreign silks and velvets were as much about economic protectionism as they were about reinforcing class divisions.

By the late Middle Ages, the effectiveness of sumptuary laws began to wane. The rising power of the merchant class and the expansion of trade routes made luxury goods more accessible, undermining the rigid social distinctions these laws sought to enforce. However, their legacy persisted in the way fashion continued to signal status and identity in European society.

The Rise of Tailoring

The medieval period marked a significant shift in how clothing was made and worn. The rise of tailoring transformed fashion from loosely draped garments to more fitted, individualized styles. This change reflected evolving tastes, advancements in textile production, and the growing influence of skilled craftspeople who elevated garment-making into an art form.

Before tailoring became widespread, most medieval clothing was constructed from rectangular pieces of fabric, folded and sewn with minimal shaping. This method was efficient, as it wasted little material, but it limited the complexity of designs. Around the 12th century, tailors began using techniques to shape fabric to the body, creating more structured and fitted garments. This innovation allowed for greater mobility, comfort, and aesthetic appeal.

The introduction of the **gore**, a triangular piece of fabric sewn into seams, was one of tailoring's key advancements. This technique allowed garments like tunics and gowns to flare out at the hem while remaining snug at the waist and chest. The result was a more flattering silhouette, which became highly desirable among both men and women. Gores also made clothing more practical, as the flared design allowed for ease of movement while maintaining a tailored appearance.

Another tailoring innovation was the use of **lacing and buttons** for fastening. These replaced older methods like pins and brooches, allowing garments to be adjusted for a closer fit. Buttons, initially expensive and reserved for the elite, became more common by the 14th century as metalworking techniques improved. The addition of laces and buttons made clothing more versatile, as garments could now be easily tightened or loosened depending on the wearer's needs.

Tailoring also introduced the concept of **layering garments** for style and functionality. Fitted undergarments, such as the **doublet** for men or the **kirtle** for women, served as a base layer. These were often made from sturdy fabrics like linen or wool and tailored to provide support. Over these, individuals wore outer garments like surcoats or houppelandes, which could be richly decorated and made from luxurious materials. This layering not only added depth and texture to medieval fashion but also allowed for adaptability to different weather conditions.

The role of tailors became increasingly important as demand for fitted clothing grew. Tailors, often organized into guilds, developed specialized skills in cutting, stitching, and fitting garments. These professionals worked closely with clients, taking measurements and crafting clothing to their exact specifications. This level of customization marked a departure from the one-size-fits-all approach of earlier periods, highlighting the growing emphasis on individuality in fashion.

Tailoring also influenced the use of **textiles**. Fabrics were now cut and pieced together in more intricate ways, requiring careful planning and precision. This led to the development of more elaborate patterns and color combinations. The practice of **parti-coloring**, where garments were made from fabrics of different colors sewn together, became a popular trend in the 14th century. This style, which often used contrasting colors on different halves of a garment, showcased the tailor's skill and the wearer's wealth.

Regional styles began to emerge as tailoring techniques spread across Europe. Italian tailors, for example, were renowned for their use of fine fabrics like silk and brocade, creating gowns with flowing lines and elegant details. In England and France, the emphasis was on structure and volume, with garments like the houppelande featuring dramatic sleeves and high collars. These regional differences reflected local tastes and resources but were united by the shared influence of tailoring.

The rise of tailoring also had social implications. Fitted clothing became a symbol of sophistication and modernity, distinguishing those who could afford tailored garments from those who relied on simpler, unshaped designs. The growing middle class, eager to emulate the nobility, turned to tailors to create garments that mimicked aristocratic styles. This demand fueled the expansion of the tailoring profession and contributed to the democratization of fashion.

Tailoring's emphasis on craftsmanship and individuality laid the groundwork for the highly structured and elaborate fashions of the Renaissance. The innovations of medieval tailors not only transformed how people dressed but also redefined the relationship between clothing and identity.

CHAPTER 4: RENAISSANCE REVIVAL

The Rebirth of Luxury Fabrics

The Renaissance was a period of transformation in Europe, and fashion was no exception. With renewed interest in art, trade, and craftsmanship, the production of luxury fabrics surged to unprecedented heights. These textiles acted as symbols of status, wealth, and the changing cultural values of the time. Advances in weaving, dyeing, and design revolutionized the way fabrics were made, traded, and worn.

Italian city-states like Florence, Venice, and Genoa became the epicenters of textile production during the Renaissance. Florence was particularly renowned for its silk industry. Wealthy families like the Medici funded silk workshops, turning the city into a hub for fine fabrics. Venetian merchants, meanwhile, imported raw silk from the East, processed it locally, and exported finished products throughout Europe. Genoa gained fame for its luxurious velvets, a fabric that came to define Renaissance fashion. The competition between these cities spurred innovation, with each vying to produce the most intricate and desirable textiles.

Velvet was one of the defining fabrics of the Renaissance. Made from silk, its plush texture and ability to absorb dye made it the ultimate luxury material. Velvet production required specialized looms and highly skilled weavers, which increased its cost and exclusivity. Genoese velvet was especially prized for its deep colors and patterns, often featuring floral motifs or geometric designs. These patterns were woven directly into the fabric using a technique called **cut-pile weaving**, creating a raised, three-dimensional effect. Velvet wasn't just used for clothing—it adorned furniture, wall hangings, and ceremonial robes, making it a status symbol both in fashion and interiors.

Brocade was another hallmark of Renaissance luxury. This fabric featured intricate patterns woven with gold or silver threads, giving it a shimmering, opulent appearance. Brocade's complexity made it expensive, and it was often reserved for the nobility and clergy. Italian artisans perfected the art of brocade weaving, drawing inspiration from Byzantine and Islamic designs. The patterns often included mythological scenes, religious symbols, or heraldic motifs, reflecting the wearer's status and affiliations. Brocade garments were heavy, not just because of the metallic threads but also due to the dense weaving, which further emphasized their richness.

The Renaissance also saw a revival of damask, a reversible fabric with elaborate patterns. Named after the city of Damascus, where it was first produced, damask was woven on draw looms that allowed for intricate designs. Renaissance damasks were typically made from silk and featured motifs inspired by nature, such as vines, flowers, and birds. Unlike brocade, damask relied on the interplay of light and shadow created by the weave, giving it a subtle elegance. It became a favorite for both clothing and home decor, symbolizing refinement and taste.

Silk itself underwent a transformation during the Renaissance. While silk had been a luxury item for centuries, the development of local production in Europe reduced its dependence on imports from the East. Italian silk weavers improved on Chinese and Byzantine techniques, creating fabrics that were not only beautiful but also durable. Silk was often combined with other fibers, such as wool or linen, to produce hybrid fabrics that offered both luster and practicality. The introduction of new dyes, such as cochineal red and indigo blue, further expanded the color palette available to silk artisans.

Trade networks were influential in the rebirth of luxury fabrics. The Silk Road, which connected Europe to Asia, continued to bring raw materials like silk and exotic dyes to European markets. At the same time, maritime trade routes established by Portuguese and Spanish explorers opened access to new resources from the Americas and India. Cochineal, a vibrant red dye derived from insects found in Mexico, became one of the most valuable exports of the New World. Its rich, long-lasting color replaced earlier red dyes like madder and kermes, transforming the way textiles were colored.

The development of advanced dyeing techniques added another layer of sophistication to Renaissance fabrics. Dyers became highly specialized artisans, often working in guilds to protect their trade secrets. Natural dyes extracted from plants, minerals, and insects were carefully processed to achieve consistent and vibrant colors. For example, woad and indigo were used to produce deep blues, while saffron and weld created yellows. Mordants like alum and iron were added to fix the dyes to the fabric and enhance their brilliance. The science of dyeing became so advanced that specific colors, such as Tyrian purple or Venetian red, became associated with particular regions or workshops.

Embroidery further elevated Renaissance textiles. Garments made from fine silk, velvet, or brocade were often adorned with intricate needlework, using gold and silver threads, pearls, and gemstones. Embroidered designs ranged from religious symbols to floral patterns, reflecting the wearer's personal tastes and social status. The **Opus Anglicanum**, a style of English embroidery, gained international fame for its intricate designs and shimmering metallic threads. Although embroidery had been practiced for centuries, the Renaissance took it to new heights, integrating it seamlessly with the luxurious fabrics of the time.

Sumptuary laws attempted to regulate the use of luxury fabrics, but their effectiveness was limited. These laws, enacted by both secular and religious authorities, sought to prevent the lower classes from dressing like the nobility. In England, for example, a 16th-century law restricted the use of velvet and brocade to the aristocracy, while merchants and commoners were limited to wool or linen. However, the growing wealth of the merchant class allowed many to skirt these restrictions, often by purchasing less ornate versions of luxurious fabrics. This led to a blending of styles and a gradual democratization of fashion.

The influence of luxury fabrics extended beyond Europe. Ottoman and Persian textiles, such as silk ikats and embroidered velvets, were highly sought after in Renaissance courts. These exotic fabrics were often used to make gowns, capes, and accessories, adding an element of global sophistication to European fashion. Italian weavers, inspired by these imports, began incorporating Eastern motifs into their designs, creating a fusion of styles that reflected the interconnectedness of the Renaissance world.

Luxury fabrics weren't just about appearance; they were also about the experience of wearing them. The tactile qualities of silk, velvet, and brocade added to their allure. Velvet's softness, silk's smoothness, and brocade's textured richness made them sensual as well as visual pleasures. This emphasis on texture marked a departure from the purely functional approach to fabric seen in earlier periods. Renaissance fashion celebrated the body, and the fabrics used were designed to enhance its movement, shape, and presence.

The Renaissance also introduced the concept of seasonal fashion, driven by the availability of certain fabrics. Lighter silks and linens were favored for summer, while heavier velvets and brocades were reserved for winter. This seasonal approach reflected both practical considerations and the increasing importance of fashion as a form of personal expression. Wealthy patrons often commissioned entire wardrobes tailored to specific times of the year, showcasing their ability to adapt to changing styles and climates.

The rebirth of luxury fabrics during the Renaissance wasn't just a matter of aesthetics; it was a reflection of the era's values. The emphasis on craftsmanship, innovation, and beauty in textiles mirrored broader cultural shifts toward humanism and individualism. These fabrics didn't just adorn bodies—they told stories about power, trade, and creativity, making them central to the fashion of the Renaissance.

Gendered Styles in Renaissance Europe

During the Renaissance, fashion became distinctly gendered, reflecting the social roles and expectations of men and women. Clothing was no longer just functional; it became a powerful way to express status, identity, and ideals of masculinity and femininity. Men's and women's clothing diverged in silhouette, materials, and decoration, emphasizing different aspects of the body and character.

Men's fashion during the Renaissance highlighted physical strength and authority. Doublets, a fitted jacket worn over a shirt, were central to men's wardrobes. These garments were tailored to accentuate the shoulders and chest, creating a triangular silhouette that symbolized power. The doublet often featured padded shoulders and was paired with **hose**, a close-fitting garment covering the legs. Hose were typically divided into upper (trunk hose) and lower sections, emphasizing the muscular shape of the legs. Materials like velvet, brocade, and fine wool were common, with bold colors and patterns reflecting confidence and vigor.

The **codpiece**, a distinctive feature of men's fashion, emerged as both a practical and symbolic garment. Initially designed to cover the gap between the two sections of hose, it became exaggerated in size and decoration over time. Codpieces were often padded, embroidered, or even adorned with jewels, drawing attention to the wearer's virility. This focus on the codpiece highlighted Renaissance ideals of masculinity, where strength, reproduction, and dominance were central themes.

Outer garments for men included cloaks and **capes**, which served both practical and decorative purposes. These pieces often featured fur linings or trim, emphasizing wealth and status. The **mantle**, a long, flowing cloak, was a favored choice for formal occasions, while shorter capes like the **beretta** were more suited to everyday wear. Accessories such as hats and gloves completed the ensemble, with wide-brimmed hats and feathered caps signaling sophistication.

Women's fashion in the Renaissance emphasized elegance, modesty, and fertility. The **gown**, or **kirtle**, was the foundational garment, featuring a fitted bodice and a full skirt that extended to the floor. Corsetry, though not as rigid as later styles, was used to shape the upper body into a cone-like silhouette, emphasizing a narrow waist. This contrast between the fitted bodice and voluminous skirt created an idealized feminine form. Sleeves were detachable, allowing women to mix and match styles. These sleeves often featured intricate slashing or puffing, revealing layers of fabric beneath.

The **farthingale**, introduced in the late Renaissance, became a hallmark of women's fashion. This undergarment consisted of a framework of hoops, originally made from whalebone or willow, sewn into a petticoat. It expanded the skirt outward, creating a bell-shaped silhouette that conveyed wealth and refinement. Farthingales varied in size and style across regions, with Spanish farthingales being more conical and French farthingales adopting a wider, drum-like shape.

Necklines for women's gowns varied based on cultural and religious norms. In Catholic regions like Spain and Italy, high necklines were common, emphasizing modesty. In contrast, French and English fashion often featured square or rounded necklines that exposed more of the chest and shoulders, symbolizing beauty and allure. Decorative collars and **partlets**, sheer fabric panels worn over the chest, allowed women to adapt their outfits to different levels of formality or modesty.

Fabrics and embellishments also differed by gender. Men's clothing was often heavier, with an emphasis on structure and bold patterns, while women's garments used lighter materials like silk and taffeta, adorned with lace, embroidery, and pearls. Jewelry was influential in women's fashion, with necklaces, brooches, and earrings highlighting their status and beauty. Hair was often styled elaborately, with jeweled nets, ribbons, and veils adding layers of ornamentation.

Both men's and women's clothing served as a visual representation of their roles in society. Men's tailored, angular garments conveyed authority and public presence, while women's flowing, decorative gowns emphasized their roles in the private and domestic spheres. These distinctions were reinforced through sumptuary laws, which dictated who could wear specific colors, fabrics, and accessories based on gender and social class.

The Spread of Italian and French Influence

The Renaissance's epicenters, Italy and France, shaped European fashion during the period, spreading their styles through trade, diplomacy, and cultural exchange. Italian and French clothing innovations influenced the way people dressed across the continent, establishing these regions as the leading arbiters of taste.

Italy's influence stemmed from its thriving city-states, particularly Florence, Venice, and Milan. These cities were renowned for their textile production and wealth, making them fertile ground for fashion innovation. Italian garments emphasized luxury and refinement, using high-quality silks, velvets, and brocades adorned with gold and silver threads. Florentine tailors were especially skilled, creating garments with intricate patterns and fine embroidery that set the standard for elegance.

Italian fashion was characterized by vivid colors and bold contrasts. Doublets, gowns, and cloaks often featured contrasting fabrics sewn together in geometric patterns, creating a striking visual effect. This style, known as **parti-coloring**, reflected Italy's appreciation for artistic experimentation. Accessories like gloves, hats, and belts were equally elaborate, often embellished with jewels or embroidery.

The **slashed style**, where outer garments were cut to reveal the fabric underneath, originated in Italy and quickly gained popularity across Europe. This technique allowed wearers to showcase the richness of their clothing layers while adding a dynamic, textured appearance. Venetian fashion, in particular, adopted slashing, incorporating it into flowing gowns and decorative sleeves.

France emerged as a dominant fashion influence in the late Renaissance, particularly under the reign of Francis I. Known for his patronage of the arts, Francis I brought Italian artisans and tailors to the French court, blending Italian craftsmanship with French aesthetics. The result was a uniquely French style that emphasized grandeur and ornamentation. French garments often featured rich fabrics like satin and damask, adorned with lace collars and cuffs.

French influence was particularly evident in the development of collars. The **ruff**, a stiff, pleated collar, became one of the most iconic features of Renaissance fashion. Initially modest in size, ruffs grew larger and more elaborate as they spread across Europe. The French court's adoption of the ruff set a trend that other monarchs and nobles followed, making it a symbol of aristocratic fashion.

Fashion spread through diplomatic marriages and court connections. When Catherine de' Medici, an Italian noblewoman, married Henry II of France, she brought Italian fashion sensibilities with her. Catherine introduced innovations like **corsets** and **perfumed gloves**, which quickly became staples of French fashion. Her influence extended beyond the court, shaping the tastes of France's nobility and spreading to other European courts.

Trade was key in disseminating Italian and French styles. Venetian merchants, who controlled key trade routes, exported luxurious textiles like silk and velvet to cities across Europe. French merchants, meanwhile, traded lace and finely woven fabrics, making these materials accessible to the wealthy elite in England, Spain, and beyond. The demand for these goods drove the establishment of local workshops, where artisans imitated Italian and French techniques.

The printing press also contributed to the spread of fashion. Illustrated pattern books, such as Cesare Vecellio's *Degli Habiti Antichi et Moderni*, showcased Italian and French styles, allowing tailors in other countries to replicate the latest trends. These books featured detailed engravings of garments, complete with descriptions of materials, patterns, and cuts, making Renaissance fashion more accessible to a broader audience.

Italian and French styles were adapted to local tastes as they spread. In Spain, for example, Italian doublets were modified to include longer sleeves and higher necklines, reflecting the country's more conservative values. In England, French ruffs were adopted with dramatic flair, becoming larger and stiffer than their continental counterparts. These regional variations highlight how Italian and French influence served as a foundation for diverse interpretations of Renaissance fashion.

Courts across Europe competed to emulate the sophistication of Italy and France. German and Flemish courts, for instance, adopted Italian tailoring techniques to create fitted garments that showcased their wealth. Polish and Hungarian nobles imported French fabrics and commissioned Italian tailors to craft their wardrobes. This widespread adoption of Italian and French styles cemented their status as leaders in Renaissance fashion.

From blending artistry with practicality, Italy and France set the tone for fashion during the Renaissance. Their emphasis on luxury, craftsmanship, and innovation defined the period and shaped the trajectory of European clothing for centuries.

CHAPTER 5: BAROQUE AND ROCOCO OPULENCE

Extravagance in the Court of Louis XIV

The court of Louis XIV at Versailles was a masterpiece of extravagance, and fashion was one of its most prominent features. Louis XIV, often called the Sun King, understood the value of clothing as a statement of power, wealth, and control. Under his reign (1643–1715), France became the epicenter of European fashion, and the court at Versailles set the standard for opulence. Fashion was not just a personal choice; it served a political function and a means of solidifying the king's authority.

Louis XIV himself embodied the ideals of Baroque fashion. He was known for his elaborate outfits made of the finest materials, including velvet, silk, and satin. His garments were often adorned with gold and silver embroidery, lace, and jewels. The king's wardrobe was meticulously curated to project his divine right to rule. He adopted the image of Apollo, the sun god, incorporating sunburst motifs into his clothing and accessories. This wasn't just vanity—it was a calculated way to connect his rule to celestial power and grandeur.

The king's love of fashion extended to his footwear. Louis XIV popularized **high-heeled shoes**, which became known as "Louis heels." These shoes, often made of red-dyed leather and embellished with intricate designs, were a symbol of status and privilege. Only those in the king's favor were permitted to wear red heels, turning footwear into a visual marker of political and social standing. The height of the heel added to the overall extravagance of Baroque fashion, elongating the silhouette and emphasizing the grandeur of the wearer.

Versailles was not just a palace; it was a stage, and clothing was a key part of the performance. Courtiers were expected to dress according to strict codes, which dictated everything from the type of fabric to the number of accessories. These regulations weren't arbitrary—they served to maintain a hierarchy within the court. Only the wealthiest and most influential nobles could afford the extravagant outfits required to keep up with the demands of court life. This ensured that power remained concentrated among those closest to the king.

One of the most distinctive elements of fashion at Versailles was the use of **lace**. French lace-making reached new heights under Louis XIV, with patterns becoming increasingly intricate and luxurious. Lace was used to adorn collars, cuffs, and bodices, adding texture and refinement to garments. Chantilly and Alençon lace, produced in France, became highly sought after, not only at court but across Europe. Louis XIV's investment in the domestic textile industry ensured that France dominated the production of luxury fabrics, further cementing its influence in fashion.

Colors in Baroque fashion were vibrant and symbolic. Louis XIV favored shades like royal blue, gold, and crimson, which conveyed wealth and authority. The dyes used to create these colors were expensive, derived from rare materials such as indigo, cochineal, and saffron. Wearing these colors signaled not only access to wealth but also allegiance to the king. In contrast, less affluent members of society were restricted to wearing muted tones, reinforcing social divisions.

The structure of Baroque garments also reflected the extravagance of the era. For men, doublets gave way to **justaucorps**, long, fitted coats worn over elaborate waistcoats. These coats featured wide cuffs, lavish embroidery, and metallic buttons. Breeches, often made from silk or velvet, were tailored to emphasize the legs, while stockings completed the look. Accessories like wigs and hats added to the overall effect, with powdered wigs becoming larger and more elaborate as the century progressed.

Women's fashion at Versailles was equally grand. Gowns were constructed with **corsets** that created a narrow waist and emphasized the bust. The skirts were voluminous, supported by panniers—hooped undergarments that extended the sides of the dress while leaving the front and back relatively flat. This exaggerated silhouette became a hallmark of Baroque fashion. Fabrics like silk and taffeta were adorned with embroidery, ribbons, and pearls, turning each gown into a work of art. The neckline was often low and square, showcasing the décolletage, while sleeves ended in flounces of lace or ruffles.

Hairstyles and headpieces were an essential part of women's fashion. The **fontange**, a tall, layered headdress named after one of Louis XIV's mistresses, became a must-have accessory. This intricate structure of ribbons, lace, and wire added height and drama to the overall look. Wigs, powdered and styled into elaborate shapes, became increasingly popular, especially as women sought to match the grandeur of their gowns.

Jewelry was another critical element of Baroque fashion at Versailles. Diamonds, pearls, and other precious stones were worn in abundance, adorning everything from necklaces and earrings to shoe buckles and hairpins. Louis XIV's court often displayed jewels not just for personal adornment but as a form of wealth on display. The king himself had an impressive collection, including the famed **Hope Diamond**, which was part of the French Crown Jewels.

The emphasis on luxury extended to every detail of court life, including accessories. Fans, gloves, and handkerchiefs were essential items for both men and women. Fans were particularly significant, as they were often decorated with painted scenes or embroidered designs that reflected the wearer's taste and sophistication. Gloves, made from soft leather or silk, were embroidered and perfumed, adding another layer of refinement to an already elaborate ensemble.

Louis XIV's court also influenced how fashion was disseminated. The king established **state-sponsored textile manufactories**, such as the Gobelins and Beauvais workshops, to produce high-quality fabrics and tapestries. These institutions not only supplied the court but also exported their products across Europe, spreading French taste and style. The king's policies encouraged innovation in weaving, dyeing, and embroidery, ensuring that France remained the leader in luxury fashion.

The court of Louis XIV set a precedent for fashion as a means of political power. By making Versailles the center of style, Louis XIV ensured that nobles spent vast amounts of money on their wardrobes, keeping them financially dependent on the crown. This strategy minimized dissent and reinforced the idea that the king was the ultimate arbiter of taste and authority. Nobles who failed to meet the court's fashion standards risked losing favor, illustrating how clothing became intertwined with politics and power.

The sheer extravagance of Louis XIV's court had a lasting impact on European fashion. His reign established France as the fashion capital of Europe, a legacy that continued well into the 18th century and beyond. The emphasis on luxury, artistry, and detail at Versailles influenced the Rococo period and set the stage for the modern fashion industry, where clothing remains both a personal and political statement.

Rococo Elegance and Ornamentation

The Rococo era, emerging in the early 18th century, took the opulence of the Baroque period and infused it with playfulness, refinement, and lightness. While Baroque fashion emphasized grandeur and structured magnificence, Rococo style leaned into delicate details, pastel colors, and elaborate ornamentation. The shift reflected broader cultural changes, as the aristocracy sought to display their wealth and sophistication through subtle yet intricate designs.

Rococo clothing was characterized by softer silhouettes and an emphasis on asymmetry. Women's gowns, such as the **robe à la française**, featured flowing backs known as **watteau pleats**, which cascaded from the shoulders to the floor, creating a sense of effortless grace. The front of the gown was more structured, with a fitted bodice shaped by corsetry and decorated with intricate embroidery, lace, and ribbons. This balance between structure and fluidity became a hallmark of Rococo elegance.

Pastel colors dominated Rococo fashion, replacing the rich jewel tones of the Baroque period. Soft shades of pink, blue, green, and ivory, often combined with gold or silver accents, created a dreamy aesthetic. These hues were enhanced by the use of fine silks and satins, which reflected light beautifully. Floral patterns, inspired by the naturalistic art of the time, were common, appearing as woven designs in fabrics or as painted embellishments on gowns.

Ornamentation reached new heights during the Rococo period. Gowns were adorned with **ruffles**, **flounces**, and **trimmings**, often layered to create texture and movement. These embellishments extended to every part of the garment, from the hem of the skirt to the sleeves and neckline. Women's sleeves were particularly elaborate, ending in tiers of lace or ruffled fabric that flared out dramatically. Necklines were often low and decorated with bows or jewels, drawing attention to the décolletage.

Men's fashion in the Rococo period, while less flamboyant than women's, was equally elegant. The **habit à la française**, a three-piece suit consisting of a coat, waistcoat, and breeches, became the standard for aristocratic men. These garments were made from luxurious fabrics like velvet or brocade and featured intricate embroidery along the edges. Waistcoats were often brightly colored or patterned, providing a striking contrast to the more subdued tones of the coat. Breeches were tailored to fit snugly, emphasizing the legs, while stockings completed the look.

Wigs continued to be an essential element of Rococo fashion for both men and women. Men's wigs were powdered and styled into neat, symmetrical shapes, often tied back with a black ribbon. Women's wigs grew increasingly elaborate, reaching towering heights and adorned with **ornaments**, **flowers**, and even miniature figurines. These hairstyles, though impractical, became a symbol of status and creativity, with the most fashionable women employing skilled hairdressers to maintain their wigs.

The Rococo period also introduced **panniers**, wide hoops worn under skirts to expand them sideways while keeping the front and back relatively flat. This exaggerated silhouette emphasized the hips and created a canvas for the detailed designs of the gown's fabric. Panniers could be modest in size for everyday wear or dramatically wide for court events and formal occasions. The use of panniers highlighted the wealth required to afford large quantities of expensive fabric.

Accessories and makeup were considered important in completing the Rococo look. Women applied powder, rouge, and patches (small decorative pieces of fabric) to their faces, enhancing their complexion while following the aesthetic of controlled artifice. Jewelry, particularly pearls, diamonds, and cameos, adorned the neck, wrists, and ears, adding sparkle to the already ornate ensembles. Shoes, often made from silk or brocade and featuring decorative buckles, were designed to complement the gown.

The Rococo style extended beyond clothing, influencing furniture, interiors, and even gardens. This integration of art and fashion created a cohesive aesthetic, where every element of aristocratic life reflected the ideals of elegance, luxury, and pleasure. Gowns often mirrored the designs found in tapestries or wallpaper, with shared motifs like garlands, shells, and pastoral scenes.

The Role of Accessories

Accessories were essential to Baroque and Rococo fashion, completing outfits and reinforcing the wearer's status, personality, and attention to detail. No outfit of the era was considered complete without carefully chosen embellishments, and the range of accessories reflected the period's love of excess and refinement.

Hats and headpieces were among the most visible accessories. In the Baroque period, men favored wide-brimmed hats, often decorated with feathers or ribbons. The **tricorne**, a hat with three sides turned up, became a defining feature of men's fashion in the late Baroque and early Rococo periods. Women's headwear evolved from simple caps to elaborate **bonnets** adorned with lace, flowers, and ribbons. These accessories weren't just decorative; they also signified the wearer's social standing and occasion, with larger and more ornate designs reserved for formal events.

Gloves were another indispensable accessory. Made from fine leather, silk, or lace, gloves conveyed elegance and sophistication. Both men and women wore gloves, but their styles differed. Men's gloves were typically plain and functional, while women's gloves were often embroidered or embellished with ribbons. Gloves also had symbolic meanings; gifting gloves was a common gesture of courtship or loyalty.

Fans became iconic during the Rococo era, serving both practical and aesthetic purposes. These folding accessories were made from materials like ivory, tortoiseshell, or wood, with panels of silk or paper painted with delicate scenes. Fans often depicted pastoral landscapes, mythological figures, or romantic vignettes, showcasing the artistic tastes of the wearer. They were not just decorative; they served as tools for flirtation and communication, with specific gestures conveying secret messages in courtly settings.

Jewelry was central to Baroque and Rococo fashion, highlighting wealth and sophistication. Diamonds were particularly prized during this period, often set into necklaces, brooches, and rings. Pearls, associated with purity and elegance, adorned everything from earrings to hairpins. **Chokers** and layered necklaces drew attention to the neckline, while bracelets added sparkle to the wrists. Cameos, carved from shells or stones, gained popularity as pendants and brooches, often depicting classical figures or sentimental scenes.

Hair accessories were another critical element of Rococo fashion, especially for women. The towering hairstyles of the period required structural support, provided by combs, pins, and frames made of wire or whalebone. These structures were often decorated with ribbons, feathers, and artificial flowers, creating a sense of whimsy and creativity. For the most extravagant occasions, women added miniature figurines or dioramas to their hair, turning their coiffures into works of art.

Shoes in the Baroque and Rococo periods were both functional and decorative. Men's shoes featured buckles made from metal or gemstones, while women's shoes were often made of brocade or silk and adorned with embroidery or ribbons. Heels became more prominent during these periods, with both men and women wearing elevated footwear to enhance their stature. Red heels, popularized by Louis XIV, remained a status symbol throughout the Rococo era.

Handkerchiefs and pomanders added subtle touches of refinement. Handkerchiefs, made from fine linen or lace, were often perfumed and carried as both a practical item and a decorative accessory. Pomanders, small containers filled with fragrant herbs or oils, were worn as necklaces or tucked into pockets. These accessories reflected the period's obsession with sensory pleasure and personal hygiene.

Belts and girdles served both functional and decorative purposes. Men's belts, often made of leather, were simple yet elegant, sometimes featuring engraved buckles. Women's girdles were more elaborate, often made from silk or velvet and embroidered with metallic threads. These accessories not only cinched the waist but also emphasized the silhouette of the garment.

The integration of accessories into Baroque and Rococo fashion showcased the era's attention to detail. Each item, from a fan to a hatpin, contributed to the overall aesthetic, reflecting the wearer's taste and ability to afford luxury. Accessories weren't just add-ons; they were essential components of an outfit, transforming clothing into an intricate and cohesive statement of style and status.

The Birth of Fashion Icons in Royal Courts

The Baroque and Rococo periods saw the emergence of fashion icons in royal courts, individuals whose styles defined the aesthetic of their time and influenced not only their peers but the broader culture of Europe. These fashion leaders were often monarchs, queens, or influential courtiers who used clothing to project power, elegance, and taste. Through their extravagant wardrobes and carefully curated public appearances, they set trends that rippled across the continent.

Louis XIV of France was one of the earliest and most influential fashion icons. Known as the Sun King, Louis understood the political and cultural power of fashion. He transformed Versailles into a hub of luxury and set strict dress codes for his court. His elaborate outfits, made of the finest fabrics and adorned with gold embroidery and jewels, symbolized his divine authority and control. His signature **high-heeled red shoes**, exclusive to the nobility, became a status symbol across Europe. By associating his personal style with grandeur and authority, Louis XIV ensured that his court dictated the fashion standards of the era.

Marie Antoinette, Queen of France during the late Rococo period, elevated the concept of a fashion icon to new heights. Her extravagant wardrobe, designed by her personal dressmaker Rose Bertin, included gowns with elaborate embroidery, wide panniers, and pastel colors. Marie Antoinette introduced trends like the **robe à la polonaise**, a gown with a draped overskirt revealing decorative underskirts. Her hairstyles were equally groundbreaking; her towering wigs, often adorned with feathers, flowers, or even miniature ships, became symbols of her influence. While her style was widely imitated, it also drew criticism, symbolizing the excesses of the French monarchy during a time of social unrest.

Elizabeth I of England, though from an earlier period, laid the groundwork for royalty as a fashion icon, and her legacy influenced Baroque and Rococo court fashion. Elizabeth's use of opulent fabrics, such as velvet and cloth of gold, and her extensive jewelry collection established the importance of visual splendor in royal fashion. Her successors in European courts adopted her approach, recognizing that clothing could communicate power, stability, and sophistication. Baroque monarchs expanded on this, incorporating even more elaborate details and integrating their personal styles into the cultural fabric of their kingdoms.

Catherine the Great of Russia adopted and adapted European styles to reinforce her image as a modernizing leader. Her court attire blended Rococo elegance with traditional Russian elements, such as fur-trimmed gowns and kokoshnik-style headdresses. Catherine commissioned European tailors to create gowns that reflected her status while subtly promoting her political reforms. Her ability to merge Russian and European aesthetics made her a fashion icon in her own right, influencing both domestic and international perceptions of Russian culture.

The role of male fashion icons during these periods should not be overlooked. Charles II of England introduced the **three-piece suit**, which became a foundational element of men's fashion. His decision to adopt this streamlined and tailored style marked a shift from the flowing robes of earlier periods to a more structured and practical look. This innovation, while understated compared to the opulence of women's fashion, represented a significant evolution in European court attire.

Madame de Pompadour, the official mistress of Louis XV, was another key figure in shaping Rococo fashion. Her influence extended beyond clothing to hairstyles, accessories, and interior design. She popularized the **pompadour hairstyle**, a voluminous updo that complemented the elaborate gowns of the period. Madame de Pompadour also championed pastel colors and floral patterns, aligning fashion with the lighter, more playful aesthetic of the Rococo era. Her tastes were immortalized in countless portraits, which spread her image and style across Europe.

The creation of fashion icons was closely tied to portraiture and other visual media. Royal courts commissioned paintings that showcased their rulers and courtiers in the latest styles. Artists like Hyacinthe Rigaud and François Boucher were important in amplifying the influence of these figures by immortalizing their looks. Rigaud's portrait of Louis XIV, for example, not only highlighted the king's opulent attire but also emphasized the connection between fashion and power. Similarly,

Boucher's portraits of Madame de Pompadour captured her elegance and taste, further cementing her status as a style leader.

Fashion icons in royal courts also influenced the development of luxury industries. Louis XIV's support of French textile manufactories, such as those producing silk in Lyon or lace in Chantilly, not only bolstered the economy but also ensured that French fashion dominated Europe. Royals and their courtiers set the demand for these luxury goods, creating a trickle-down effect that spread styles to the bourgeoisie and eventually the working class. This connection between royalty and industry established the foundation for modern fashion systems, where trends originate with elites and permeate society.

Royal courts were also sites of fierce competition among courtiers to gain attention through their attire. Nobles vied to outshine each other at events such as balls, masques, and fêtes, often spending fortunes on clothing and accessories. These displays of extravagance were not merely about vanity; they were calculated efforts to secure favor and influence within the court. A well-dressed courtier could catch the king or queen's eye, leading to political and social advancement. This dynamic made fashion an essential aspect of court life and elevated the importance of personal style.

The influence of fashion icons extended beyond their own courts through diplomatic marriages and alliances. When Marie de' Medici married Henry IV of France, she brought Italian fashion to the French court, introducing new fabrics and designs. Similarly, the marriage of Maria Theresa of Austria to Louis XIV strengthened ties between France and the Habsburg Empire, facilitating the exchange of fashion trends. These unions often led to a blending of styles, with elements from different cultures incorporated into royal wardrobes.

Accessories were a vital part of how fashion icons established their status. The towering wigs of the Rococo period, the richly adorned hats of the Baroque era, and the jeweled necklaces worn by monarchs all served to enhance the wearer's appearance. Accessories were carefully chosen to complement the overall ensemble and reinforce the themes of power, luxury, and refinement. For example, Louis XIV's red-heeled shoes were more than just footwear—they were a statement of exclusivity and authority.

The legacy of these fashion icons can be seen in the way their styles continued to influence later periods. The structured elegance of Baroque fashion and the playful extravagance of Rococo designs laid the groundwork for subsequent movements, including the Neoclassical and Romantic styles. The central role of monarchs and courtiers in defining fashion also prefigured the celebrity culture of the modern era, where public figures dictate trends through their personal choices.

The birth of fashion icons in royal courts during the Baroque and Rococo periods was more than a matter of personal style. These individuals used clothing as a tool of communication, wielding their influence to shape cultural and political landscapes.

CHAPTER 6: REVOLUTIONARY SIMPLICITY

The Impact of the French Revolution on Dress

The French Revolution (1789–1799) transformed every aspect of French society, including fashion. Clothing, once a symbol of aristocratic privilege, became a powerful expression of political ideology and social change. The Revolution uprooted centuries-old traditions of opulence and hierarchy, replacing them with simplicity and egalitarianism. What people wore reflected not just their status but their political allegiances, values, and vision for the future of France.

Before the Revolution, fashion had been defined by the **lavish excesses of the aristocracy**. The court of Louis XVI at Versailles was a world of brocade gowns, powdered wigs, and jewel-encrusted accessories. However, as the Revolution gained momentum, these symbols of wealth and privilege became dangerous to wear. The extravagant styles of the monarchy and nobility came to represent the inequality that fueled revolutionary fervor. To avoid persecution, many aristocrats abandoned their finery for more modest attire.

The rise of **Revolutionary fashion** marked a stark departure from the styles of the Ancien régime. The most iconic change was the rejection of powdered wigs and elaborate hairstyles. Revolutionary men and women favored natural hair or simple cuts. For men, the **queue** hairstyle—a short, tied-back ponytail—replaced the elaborate powdered periwigs of the aristocracy. Women often let their hair fall naturally or styled it in loose curls, emulating ancient Roman and Greek figures that symbolized republican ideals.

Men's clothing shifted dramatically. The **knee breeches**, or culottes, worn by aristocrats were replaced by long trousers, a style associated with the working class. The term **sans-culottes**, literally "without breeches," became synonymous with revolutionaries. This change wasn't merely aesthetic—it was a political statement. Trousers symbolized solidarity with the common people and defiance of aristocratic privilege. Men also adopted plain, dark coats and waistcoats, reflecting a rejection of the vibrant colors and ornate embroidery that had previously dominated fashion.

Women's fashion also reflected Revolutionary ideals. The **chemise gown**, a loose-fitting, lightweight garment, became popular among women who wanted to distance themselves from the rigid corsetry and heavy fabrics of the Ancien régime. Made of simple cotton or muslin, the chemise gown was inspired by the classical drapery of ancient Greece and Rome. Its simplicity and natural silhouette symbolized the newfound emphasis on liberty, equality, and fraternity. These gowns often featured high waistlines, short sleeves, and minimal embellishment, contrasting sharply with the structured, layered dresses of the past.

Colors in Revolutionary dress carried political significance. The **tricolor cockade**, a rosette of blue, white, and red, became an essential accessory for both men and women. It was worn on hats, lapels, or dresses to demonstrate loyalty to the Revolution. Blue, white, and red represented the ideals of liberty, equality, and fraternity, and failure to wear the cockade could be seen as a sign of counter-revolutionary sympathies. Other colors associated with royalty, such as gold and purple, fell out of favor, replaced by more somber tones that reflected the austere mood of the period.

Fashion also incorporated **symbolic motifs** that celebrated Revolutionary values. Phrygian caps, or **liberty caps**, became a defining accessory of the era. These red, conical hats were modeled after the caps worn by freed slaves in ancient Rome, symbolizing emancipation and freedom. Revolutionaries often wore liberty caps adorned with the tricolor cockade, further emphasizing their commitment to the cause. The cap was not just a piece of clothing; it was a visual declaration of loyalty to the Revolution.

In addition to clothing, accessories were common in Revolutionary fashion. The **cravat**, a type of neckwear, became a symbol of personal style among men. While aristocratic cravats had been elaborate and heavily starched, Revolutionary cravats were simpler, often made of plain black or white fabric. For women, jewelry also carried political meaning. Necklaces and earrings featuring symbols like the liberty cap, the guillotine, or the Revolutionary calendar became popular. These pieces were often crafted from less expensive materials, reflecting the egalitarian values of the time.

The Revolution's emphasis on equality influenced not only the styles of clothing but also the materials used. Fabrics such as silk, long associated with the aristocracy, were replaced by more accessible and practical materials like wool, linen, and cotton. Cotton, in particular, became a symbol of the Revolution, as it was lightweight, affordable, and easy to produce. This shift democratized fashion, making it more accessible to the broader population.

Revolutionary dress was also used to enforce social and political conformity. During the Reign of Terror (1793–1794), clothing became a matter of survival. Wearing the wrong outfit or accessory could lead to accusations of counter-revolutionary activity. The revolutionary tribunal scrutinized appearances, and those who appeared too aristocratic risked imprisonment or execution. Even minor details, such as the fabric or cut of a garment, could be interpreted as a statement against the Revolution.

Certain groups within the Revolution developed their own distinct styles. The **Jacobins**, one of the most radical factions, adopted austere and somber clothing to reflect their disdain for aristocratic excess. By contrast, the **Incroyables and Merveilleuses**, a group of young aristocratic men and women, deliberately flouted Revolutionary norms with exaggerated and flamboyant styles. These "Incredibles" wore oversized cravats, long coats, and high collars, while the "Marvelous Women" favored sheer gowns, extravagant wigs, and sandals inspired by classical antiquity.

Their fashion was a form of rebellion against the strictures of Revolutionary society, highlighting the tension between freedom and conformity.

The French Revolution also marked the beginning of **politicized mass fashion**. For the first time, clothing was used to create a shared national identity. Uniforms became a key element of this effort. Revolutionary soldiers wore standardized outfits featuring the tricolor and liberty cap, reinforcing their unity and commitment to the cause. Civil servants and officials also adopted uniforms, signaling the rise of a new meritocratic order where rank was determined by service rather than birthright.

Artists and writers documented the changing styles of the Revolution, further cementing their significance. Jacques-Louis David, the Revolution's leading painter, captured the aesthetic of the era in works like *The Death of Marat*. His depictions of simple, unadorned clothing in classical poses helped shape public perceptions of Revolutionary fashion. Meanwhile, satirical cartoons mocked the extremes of both austerity and excess, illustrating the cultural battles being fought through clothing.

The impact of the French Revolution on dress extended beyond France. Neighboring countries adopted elements of Revolutionary fashion, particularly the simpler silhouettes and fabrics. The rejection of aristocratic excess resonated with reform movements across Europe, influencing the transition to the Neoclassical styles of the early 19th century. The Revolution demonstrated that fashion could be a powerful force for political expression and social change, reshaping not only how people dressed but also how they thought about clothing and identity.

Neoclassicism and the Empire Silhouette

The French Revolution gave rise to Neoclassicism in fashion, an aesthetic movement inspired by the art and ideals of ancient Greece and Rome. This shift was not accidental; it was deeply connected to the revolutionary values of simplicity, equality, and a return to rationality. Clothing became more streamlined and symbolic, rejecting the ornate excesses of the ancien régime in favor of classical elegance.

The **Empire silhouette**, which emerged during the late 1790s and became dominant in the early 19th century, was a direct result of this Neoclassical influence. This silhouette featured a high waistline just below the bust, with the rest of the gown falling loosely to the floor. It created a columnar effect, echoing the shapes of Greco-Roman statues. The lack of restrictive corsetry and heavy layers reflected a new appreciation for natural lines and freedom of movement, aligning with the Revolutionary ideals of liberty and egalitarianism.

Women's gowns were made from lightweight fabrics like muslin, cotton, and fine linen, which draped softly over the body. These materials, often white or pastel-colored, enhanced the classical aesthetic by mimicking the simplicity of ancient garments. White became particularly popular because it symbolized purity and a break from the extravagance of pre-Revolutionary fashion. Subtle embellishments such as embroidery, lace, or small ribbons added texture without overpowering the overall simplicity of the design.

Neoclassical gowns were often inspired by archaeological discoveries of the time, such as the ruins of Pompeii and the Parthenon. The popularity of **watteau pleats**, high waistlines, and short sleeves can be traced to these discoveries, as artists and designers sought to recreate the elegance of ancient attire. Accessories like shawls, often patterned with classical motifs, became essential additions to these gowns, adding layers while maintaining the overall aesthetic.

Hairstyles during this period also embraced classical inspiration. Women wore their hair in simple buns or loose curls, often accessorized with ribbons, combs, or bands that mimicked the laurel wreaths of antiquity. Men's hairstyles became similarly restrained, favoring short, natural cuts over the elaborate wigs of the previous century. These choices reflected a broader cultural rejection of aristocratic excess and a newfound emphasis on rationality and order.

Men's fashion underwent its own transformation under Neoclassical influence. The heavily embroidered coats and breeches of the aristocracy gave way to **tailored suits** consisting of fitted trousers, waistcoats, and long coats. The emphasis shifted from decoration to fit and function, mirroring the simplicity and practicality of the times. Dark, somber colors like black, brown, and navy replaced the bright, opulent hues of the past, emphasizing restraint and professionalism.

Military uniforms also influenced Neoclassical fashion. The Empire silhouette, for instance, echoed the straight lines of Napoleonic uniforms, which were themselves influenced by Roman military attire. Epaulettes, brass buttons, and high collars found their way into civilian fashion, creating a subtle connection between the citizen and the state. This blending of classical and martial aesthetics reinforced the era's emphasis on civic duty and national pride.

Shoes and accessories complemented the Neoclassical look. Flat, slipper-like shoes made of leather or satin replaced the heeled footwear of earlier periods. These shoes often featured simple bows or ribbons and were designed to be both practical and elegant. Gloves, essential for formal occasions, were made from fine leather or silk and extended to the elbow for women. Reticules, small drawstring bags, became a popular accessory for women, replacing the cumbersome pockets of earlier periods.

Jewelry during the Neoclassical era also drew heavily from ancient motifs. Cameos, featuring profiles of classical figures or mythological scenes, were worn as brooches, necklaces, or bracelets. Gold and pearls were favored over the extravagant gemstones of the Baroque and Rococo periods, reinforcing the era's emphasis on refinement over opulence.

The simplicity of the Empire silhouette and Neoclassical fashion reflected the changing social order. With the fall of the monarchy, clothing was no longer a tool for displaying aristocratic privilege. Instead, it became a means of expressing shared values and aspirations. The Neoclassical aesthetic was accessible, practical, and democratic, aligning with the ideals of the Revolution while paving the way for the modern fashion industry.

The Democratization of Fashion

The French Revolution catalyzed the democratization of fashion, breaking down centuries-old barriers that had kept luxurious clothing exclusive to the aristocracy. As the Revolution dismantled the rigid social hierarchies of the ancien régime, fashion followed suit, becoming more accessible to the broader population. This shift wasn't just about affordability—it was a cultural realignment that redefined how people related to clothing and personal identity.

Before the Revolution, fashion had been dominated by the aristocracy. Sumptuary laws and the cost of luxury materials ensured that only the nobility could afford the latest styles. The Revolution changed this dynamic by rejecting these symbols of privilege. Fabrics like silk and brocade, long associated with royalty, fell out of favor, replaced by affordable and practical materials like cotton and linen. These changes made fashionable clothing accessible to the emerging middle class, signaling a shift in the fashion industry.

One of the key drivers of democratization was the rise of **ready-to-wear clothing**. While bespoke tailoring remained important, Revolutionary ideals of equality encouraged the production of simpler garments that could be made quickly and in larger quantities. Workshops began producing standardized clothing, such as chemise gowns and trousers, that required minimal tailoring. This approach allowed more people to participate in fashion without the cost of custom-made garments.

The emphasis on practicality also influenced men's clothing. The adoption of trousers, waistcoats, and simple coats as everyday wear for all classes blurred the lines between aristocratic and working-class styles. These garments, often made from sturdy fabrics like wool or twill, were durable, affordable, and easy to maintain. The simplicity of these designs reflected the egalitarian values of the Revolution, which sought to minimize distinctions between social classes.

The spread of **fashion publications** further accelerated the democratization process. Magazines like *Le Journal des Dames et des Modes* featured illustrations of the latest trends, making them accessible to a wider audience. While these styles were still aspirational for many, the availability of fashion plates allowed people to adapt and imitate high-end designs using more affordable materials. The Revolution's emphasis on education and literacy meant that more people could access these publications, expanding their influence.

Textile production also underwent significant changes during this period. The Revolution disrupted traditional supply chains, encouraging the development of domestic industries. Factories began producing cotton fabrics on a larger scale, reducing costs and increasing availability. French cotton became a staple of Revolutionary fashion, symbolizing both practicality and national pride. This shift laid the groundwork for the Industrial Revolution, which would later transform the global textile industry.

The rise of **tailoring guilds** and independent artisans contributed to the democratization of fashion. These professionals began catering to the needs of the middle class, offering affordable yet stylish options. Tailors and dressmakers adapted high-fashion trends for their clients, creating a bridge between aristocratic elegance and everyday practicality. This accessibility allowed a broader range of people to engage with fashion as a form of self-expression.

Accessories also became more accessible during this period. While aristocrats had once adorned themselves with diamonds and gold, Revolutionary ideals encouraged simpler, symbolic adornments. The tricolor cockade, for example, was worn by citizens of all classes, reinforcing a sense of unity and shared purpose. Other accessories, such as reticules, gloves, and shawls, became widely available in less expensive materials, allowing more people to participate in the trends of the time.

The development of **uniforms** further exemplified the democratization of fashion. Revolutionary soldiers and civil servants wore standardized clothing, emphasizing equality and service to the state. These uniforms were often adapted for civilian use, influencing everyday styles. The blending of military and civilian fashion reinforced the idea that clothing could reflect collective values rather than individual wealth.

The rise of fashion as a **mass phenomenon** during the French Revolution laid the foundation for modern consumer culture. By making clothing more accessible and emphasizing shared values over exclusivity, the Revolution transformed fashion into a democratic and dynamic industry. This shift not only reflected the social changes of the era but also set the stage for the innovations of the 19th and 20th centuries.

CHAPTER 7: THE VICTORIAN ERA

Crinolines and Corsets

The Victorian era, spanning from 1837 to 1901, was a time of dramatic changes in fashion, with crinolines and corsets defining the silhouette of women's clothing. These garments weren't just about appearance; they were deeply tied to the social norms, technological advancements, and cultural values of the time. Together, crinolines and corsets created the hourglass figure that symbolized femininity and respectability in Victorian society.

Corsets were an essential foundation garment for Victorian women. Made from sturdy materials like cotton, satin, or silk, corsets were reinforced with whalebone, steel, or cording to provide structure. They were laced tightly at the back or front to mold the torso into the desired shape, creating a narrow waist while lifting and supporting the bust. The resulting silhouette was highly stylized, emphasizing a small waist contrasted by full skirts or broad shoulders, depending on the era.

Corsets weren't just about aesthetics; they were tied to social expectations of femininity. A narrow waist signaled discipline, self-control, and adherence to societal norms. Women were expected to maintain a polished appearance, and corsets helped achieve the ideal figure. However, the tight lacing required to achieve extremely small waists became controversial, with critics arguing that it caused health problems such as difficulty breathing, compressed organs, and fainting spells.

Despite these criticisms, corsets were almost universally worn by women of all classes. Wealthier women could afford custom-made corsets, tailored to their exact measurements and made from luxurious fabrics. Middle- and working-class women wore simpler versions, often purchased from local dressmakers or ready-made from department stores as mass production became common. While the quality and decoration varied, the purpose remained the same: to shape the body into the socially acceptable ideal.

The invention of **metal eyelets** in the early 19th century made corsets more durable and allowed for tighter lacing without damaging the fabric. This innovation coincided with the growing popularity of the hourglass figure, encouraging even more dramatic waist reduction. Corsets were often paired with **bust improvers** or padding to enhance the bustline further, creating a balanced silhouette that emphasized the upper body.

The crinoline, introduced in the mid-19th century, transformed the lower half of the Victorian silhouette. Before crinolines, women relied on multiple layers of heavy petticoats to create the full skirts that were fashionable at the time. These layers were cumbersome, hot, and difficult to manage. The crinoline changed all of this. Made from steel hoops connected by fabric tapes, the crinoline provided a lightweight and structured alternative to layered petticoats. It allowed skirts to reach dramatic widths, often spanning several feet in diameter.

The adoption of crinolines was widespread, as they offered several practical advantages. The lightweight structure reduced the need for excessive layers, making movement easier and reducing the weight women had to carry. Crinolines also provided better ventilation, which was a relief in the hot and crowded environments of Victorian homes and social gatherings. However, their size made navigating narrow spaces challenging, and they were occasionally hazardous. Stories of crinolines catching fire near open flames or becoming entangled in machinery highlight the risks of this fashion innovation.

Crinolines weren't static in design. Early versions, introduced in the 1850s, were bell-shaped, with the fullness distributed evenly around the skirt. By the 1860s, the shape began to shift, with more volume concentrated at the back. This evolution reflected changing tastes and the increasing emphasis on a pronounced bustle, which would dominate the later Victorian silhouette. Crinolines also became more elaborate over time, with multiple layers of steel hoops or additional fabric ruffles to enhance their appearance.

The **social significance of crinolines** was as important as their physical structure. Their size and extravagance signaled wealth and status, as only women who didn't have to work could wear such impractical garments. A crinoline skirt required large amounts of fabric, often made from fine materials like silk or velvet, and was decorated with embroidery, lace, or fringe. The time and expense involved in maintaining such a wardrobe reinforced the idea that crinolines were a luxury reserved for the upper and middle classes.

However, crinolines were not exclusively for the elite. As mass production and industrialization made fabric and steel more affordable, crinolines became accessible to a wider audience. Working-class women adapted the style to fit their needs, opting for smaller, less expensive versions that were easier to manage. The widespread availability of crinolines highlighted the democratization of fashion during the Victorian era, where styles previously reserved for the wealthy became attainable for others.

Despite their popularity, crinolines faced criticism and satire. They were often mocked in cartoons and literature for their impracticality and the way they exaggerated the female form. Critics argued that crinolines were a symbol of vanity and excess, while others saw them as a visual representation of women's restricted roles in society. The expansive skirts made it physically difficult for women to move freely or engage in labor, reinforcing the expectation that their place was in the domestic sphere.

By the late 1860s, crinolines began to decline in popularity, replaced by the **bustle**. This new silhouette shifted the volume of the skirt entirely to the back, creating a more elongated and dramatic shape. Corsets, however, remained central to women's fashion throughout the Victorian era and beyond. Their design continued to evolve, with the introduction of the **spoon busk**, a curved steel plate at the front of the corset, which provided additional support and emphasized the waistline.

The persistence of corsets reflected their versatility and cultural significance. They adapted to changing styles, from the exaggerated hourglass figures of the mid-Victorian era to the straighter, slimmer lines of the late Victorian period. Corsets became shorter and more flexible, accommodating the active lifestyles of women who participated in cycling or sports while still adhering to societal expectations of modesty and femininity.

Toward the end of the Victorian era, reform movements began challenging the dominance of corsets and crinolines. Critics argued that these garments restricted women's health and freedom, advocating for more natural and practical styles. The **rational dress movement** emerged, promoting looser-fitting clothing that allowed for greater mobility. While these ideas gained traction, corsets and structured garments remained deeply embedded in Victorian culture, reflecting the era's complex relationship with fashion, morality, and gender roles.

The interplay between crinolines and corsets defined the Victorian silhouette, creating a visual language that spoke to the values and aspirations of the time. These garments weren't just clothing; they were symbols of identity, status, and the evolving role of women in society. Their influence extended far beyond the Victorian era, shaping the development of fashion and leaving a lasting legacy in the history of clothing design.

Mourning Dress and Social Codes

Mourning dress in the Victorian era was a highly regulated and deeply symbolic aspect of fashion, reflecting both personal grief and societal expectations. Queen Victoria's prolonged mourning for Prince Albert after his death in 1861 set the tone for an entire culture of mourning attire. Her choice to wear black for the remainder of her life established mourning dress as a central feature of Victorian social codes, influencing people across all classes.

Black was the dominant color of mourning, symbolizing sorrow and solemnity. Women wore mourning dresses made from matte fabrics like crepe, which lacked shine and conveyed humility. These dresses were often unadorned, with minimal decoration to reflect the wearer's subdued state. Lace, if used, was black and understated, avoiding the elaborate embellishments typical of Victorian fashion. Jewelry was similarly somber, with materials like jet, onyx, or vulcanite replacing the sparkling gemstones worn in normal times.

The rules of mourning were strict, particularly for women. Widows were expected to adhere to a hierarchy of mourning periods. **Deep mourning**, lasting for at least a year and a day, required plain black garments and veils of crape or gauze to cover the face. After this period, women transitioned to **half-mourning**, during which shades like gray, lavender, or mauve were permitted, along with more decorative details. Men's mourning attire was less elaborate, typically consisting of a black suit, cravat, and gloves.

Mourning dress extended beyond the immediate family to include relatives and close friends of the deceased. These social codes were enforced not only by etiquette manuals but also by societal pressure. Failing to observe proper mourning attire could lead to public criticism or social ostracism, as it was seen as disrespectful to both the deceased and the community. Mourning dress thus became a visible marker of social compliance and familial duty.

The rise of mourning attire created a thriving industry. Specialized shops and department stores catered to the demand for mourning clothing and accessories. Widows and other mourners could purchase ready-made mourning garments, making it easier to adhere to societal expectations. Mourning jewelry, often crafted from black jet or featuring locks of the deceased's hair, became a way to honor loved ones while following fashion trends.

The rigid expectations around mourning dress also highlighted the gendered nature of Victorian social codes. Women bore the primary burden of mourning attire, with widows often expected to remain in black for years or even the rest of their lives. These expectations reinforced societal roles, positioning women as the emotional caretakers of the family and community.

While mourning dress allowed individuals to publicly express grief, it also became a tool of control, regulating behavior and appearance. Over time, criticism of the elaborate mourning culture emerged, with some viewing it as excessive or performative. Despite this, mourning dress remained a powerful symbol of Victorian values, blending personal sentiment with social obligation.

Industrialization and Mass Production

The Victorian era was a time of rapid industrialization, and the fashion industry was deeply transformed by the innovations of this period. Mass production revolutionized the way clothing was made, distributed, and consumed, making fashion more accessible to a broader segment of society. This shift marked a departure from the custom, hand-crafted garments of earlier periods, as new technologies and manufacturing processes reshaped every aspect of the industry.

The invention of the **sewing machine** in the mid-19th century was one of the most significant advancements in clothing production. Machines like those developed by Isaac Singer drastically reduced the time it took to sew garments, increasing efficiency and lowering costs. Tailors and seamstresses could now produce clothing faster than ever before, paving the way for the rise of ready-to-wear fashion. By the late Victorian period, sewing machines had become common in both workshops and private homes, further democratizing clothing production.

Textile manufacturing also experienced a dramatic transformation. The introduction of power looms and mechanized spinning machines allowed factories to produce fabrics in unprecedented quantities. Cotton, wool, and silk were processed on an industrial scale, making these materials more affordable and widely available. The textile mills of Britain's industrial heartland became global leaders, exporting fabrics to markets around the world. This accessibility to materials drove the expansion of fashion for the middle and working classes, who could now afford garments made from quality fabrics.

Mass production extended to all aspects of fashion, including accessories. Shoes, hats, and gloves, once made by hand in small workshops, were now produced in factories. Advances in mechanization allowed for consistent quality and standardized sizing, making these items more affordable. Even corsets, a staple of Victorian fashion, were mass-produced using new technologies that incorporated steel stays and metal eyelets.

Department stores emerged as a direct result of industrialized production, changing the way people shopped for clothing. Stores like Harrods in London and Le Bon Marché in Paris offered a wide range of ready-to-wear garments, fabrics, and accessories under one roof. These establishments introduced fixed pricing, replacing the traditional practice of haggling, and made shopping a more accessible and enjoyable experience. They also catered to the growing middle class, who sought fashionable yet affordable clothing that reflected their aspirations.

Mass production also led to the rise of fashion catalogs. Companies like Sears, Roebuck & Co. distributed catalogs that allowed customers to browse and order clothing from the comfort of their homes. These catalogs featured detailed illustrations and descriptions, providing access to fashion for rural and remote customers who could not visit urban department stores. This innovation further expanded the reach of mass-produced fashion, connecting people across geographic and social boundaries.

The industrialization of fashion had a profound impact on women's clothing. Ready-to-wear garments became increasingly popular, offering women more convenience and choice. Dresses, skirts, and blouses were available in standardized sizes, eliminating the need for custom tailoring in many cases. However, industrialization also created new challenges. Factory-made clothing often lacked the quality and individuality of bespoke garments, leading to concerns about uniformity and loss of craftsmanship.

Children's clothing also benefited from mass production. Prior to industrialization, children often wore smaller versions of adult garments. The availability of ready-made clothing introduced designs specifically tailored to children's needs, such as looser fits and durable materials. This change reflected broader societal shifts, as Victorian ideals of childhood placed greater emphasis on play and education.

While industrialization brought many benefits, it also raised ethical concerns. Factory work was often grueling and poorly paid, with long hours and unsafe conditions. Many workers in the fashion industry were women and children, who faced exploitation and limited opportunities for advancement. The harsh realities of factory life stood in stark contrast to the elegance of Victorian fashion, creating a disconnect between production and consumption.

The mass production of clothing also had environmental consequences. The demand for cheap materials and rapid production led to overuse of natural resources, such as water and land for cotton cultivation. Chemical dyes, introduced during the Victorian period, revolutionized fashion with vibrant, long-lasting colors but also introduced pollution to waterways. Factories discharged waste into rivers, affecting ecosystems and communities.

Despite these challenges, industrialization fundamentally reshaped the relationship between people and fashion. The ability to produce clothing on a large scale democratized style, breaking down barriers between social classes and creating a more inclusive industry. While the wealthy continued to wear custom-made garments, the middle and working classes embraced ready-to-wear fashion as a way to participate in the trends of the era.

Toward the end of the Victorian period, the fashion industry had fully embraced industrialization. The innovations of this era laid the foundation for the global fashion industry, establishing systems of production, distribution, and consumption that continue to influence the way clothing is made and worn today.

CHAPTER 8: THE BIRTH OF MODERN FASHION

The Rise of Haute Couture

During and just after the Victorian period, haute couture established itself as a transformative force in fashion, with Paris becoming the unrivaled capital of luxury and innovation. The Victorian era's rigid social structures and emphasis on propriety shaped the development of haute couture, as wealthy clients sought clothing that reflected their status while adhering to the strict norms of the time.

The roots of haute couture in the Victorian period are deeply tied to **Charles Frederick Worth**, an Englishman who moved to Paris in 1845. By 1858, Worth had founded his own fashion house, the Maison Worth, in collaboration with Otto Bobergh. Worth's approach to fashion was unprecedented. He broke away from the tradition of clients dictating designs to their dressmakers. Instead, he crafted his own artistic vision and invited clients to choose from his creations. This shift marked the beginning of designers as auteurs, responsible for shaping the trends of their time.

Worth's influence was profound. He introduced the concept of presenting collections on live models, an innovation that set the standard for how fashion would be showcased. These presentations, held in opulent salons, allowed clients to visualize how garments would look when worn. The idea of the "fashion show" was born, creating a system where designers controlled both the design and presentation of their work.

Victorian haute couture thrived on the era's obsession with detail and ornamentation. Garments were often lavishly decorated with embroidery, lace, and beading. Dresses featured intricate pleating, ruching, and layered fabrics, reflecting the Victorian love of embellishment. Worth's designs, in particular, highlighted his mastery of textiles, using luxurious materials like silk, velvet, and brocade. His gowns often included dramatic crinolines and bustles, which were essential elements of Victorian fashion.

The **crinoline** became a hallmark of mid-Victorian haute couture. This voluminous, bell-shaped skirt, supported by a framework of steel hoops, allowed designers to create dramatic silhouettes. It was both a symbol of elegance and a marker of social status, as only wealthy women could afford such elaborate garments. However, the crinoline also had practical drawbacks—it was cumbersome and could be dangerous, especially in crowded spaces or near open flames. Designers like Worth adapted their styles to the changing needs of their clients, eventually replacing the crinoline with the **bustle**, which shifted volume to the back of the dress.

The Victorian period also saw the rise of specialized **atelier work**, where skilled artisans focused on specific aspects of garment construction. For example, embroidery ateliers produced intricate hand-stitched patterns, while lace-makers created delicate trims and inserts. These workshops, often located in Paris, became integral to the haute couture industry. The emphasis on craftsmanship ensured that every garment was a masterpiece, tailored to the exact measurements and preferences of the client.

Haute couture during this time catered primarily to the upper echelons of society. The Industrial Revolution had created unprecedented wealth, and newly affluent industrialists sought to emulate the aristocracy through their clothing. Parisian couture houses became pilgrimage sites for wealthy clients from across Europe and the United States. The **House of Worth**, in particular, attracted royalty, including Empress Eugénie of France, who was one of Worth's most loyal patrons. Her endorsement elevated his reputation, making his designs the epitome of sophistication and prestige.

The role of haute couture in Victorian society extended beyond aesthetics. Clothing was a powerful symbol of identity and status. For women, their attire signified their position in the social hierarchy and adhered to strict codes of modesty and femininity. Haute couture offered a way to navigate these expectations while expressing individuality within the confines of societal norms. Designers like Worth understood this duality, creating garments that balanced innovation with tradition.

The fashion industry during the Victorian period was deeply influenced by **historicism**, a trend that drew inspiration from the past. Designers often incorporated elements from previous centuries, such as Renaissance or Rococo styles, into their creations. This fascination with historical references resonated with Victorian ideals, which prized tradition and continuity. Worth was particularly adept at blending historical motifs with contemporary fashion, creating gowns that felt timeless yet modern.

As haute couture evolved in the late Victorian period, new silhouettes emerged. The **Princess line**, introduced in the 1870s, abandoned the use of a defined waistline, creating a sleek, vertical silhouette. This style, which emphasized the natural curves of the body, represented a departure from the heavily structured garments of earlier decades. Designers also began experimenting with color and texture, using innovations in dyeing techniques to produce vibrant, richly hued fabrics.

Transportation advances during the Victorian era were important in the globalization of haute couture. The expansion of railways and steamships allowed clients to travel to Paris more easily, and the telegraph enabled swift communication between designers and their patrons. As a result, Parisian fashion began to influence styles far beyond France. Wealthy American women, for instance, became avid consumers of haute couture, commissioning gowns from designers like Worth and later showcasing them at social events in New York and Newport.

The dissemination of fashion was further aided by the rise of **fashion journalism**. Publications like *La Mode Illustrée* and *Harper's Bazaar* provided detailed illustrations and descriptions of the latest couture designs, allowing women who could not travel to Paris to stay informed about trends. These magazines often featured the work of leading designers, reinforcing the dominance of Parisian haute couture.

Haute couture also responded to the technological innovations of the Victorian era. The development of the **sewing machine**, for example, revolutionized garment construction. While couture pieces remained handmade, the sewing machine allowed for faster production of undergarments and simpler items, freeing up skilled artisans to focus on the intricate details of couture gowns. Advances in textile manufacturing also introduced new fabrics, such as chemically treated silks and velvets, which expanded the possibilities for design.

As the Victorian period transitioned into the **Edwardian era**, haute couture retained its importance but began to adapt to changing tastes. The elaborate, heavily structured garments of the mid-Victorian period gave way to lighter, more fluid styles. However, the principles of haute couture—individualized design, meticulous craftsmanship, and artistic innovation—remained constant. Designers continued to push boundaries, experimenting with new silhouettes and embellishments while maintaining the exclusivity that defined the industry.

The House of Worth

The **House of Worth**, founded in Paris in 1858 by Charles Frederick Worth, was influential in the birth of modern fashion. Worth revolutionized the way clothing was designed and marketed, moving fashion from a purely functional necessity to an art form and a symbol of status. His methods not only set the standard for haute couture but also redefined the relationship between designer and client.

Before Worth, dressmakers primarily fulfilled the requests of their clients, creating garments based on the buyer's instructions. Worth rejected this model. Instead, he designed complete collections of clothing, offering his vision for what women should wear. Clients would visit his opulent salon, view pre-designed pieces modeled on live mannequins, and select garments to be custom-fitted to their measurements. This system, groundbreaking at the time, shifted creative control from the client to the designer, establishing the foundation for modern fashion houses.

The Maison Worth quickly became synonymous with luxury and innovation. Worth's designs were distinctive for their dramatic silhouettes, luxurious fabrics, and intricate detailing. He mastered the art of combining traditional craftsmanship with innovative techniques, producing garments that were both elegant and trend-setting. His use of lavish textiles, such as silk, satin, and velvet, underscored the exclusivity of his creations. He worked closely with textile manufacturers to produce custom fabrics, ensuring that his designs were truly unique.

One of Worth's most significant contributions was his embrace of **seasonal collections**. Each season, he introduced new designs that reflected current tastes and societal changes. This approach kept his work fresh and desirable, encouraging repeat visits from his wealthy clientele. It also introduced the concept of fashion as a dynamic and ever-evolving industry.

The House of Worth thrived on its association with royalty and the upper classes. Worth's most prominent patron was **Empress Eugénie**, wife of Napoleon III, who became a loyal client and an influential supporter. Her endorsement of Worth's designs elevated his reputation and attracted an elite clientele from across Europe and the United States. These clients, eager to showcase their status and wealth, willingly paid premium prices for bespoke garments.

Worth's influence extended beyond individual designs to the broader fashion industry. His success inspired other designers to open their own houses, following his model of creativity and exclusivity. He was also instrumental in defining the hierarchy of the fashion industry, placing the designer at its pinnacle. By positioning himself as both an artist and a businessman, Worth blurred the lines between commerce and creativity.

The structure of the House of Worth reflected the growing complexity of the fashion industry during the late 19th century. Worth employed skilled artisans in specialized **ateliers**, each focusing on a specific aspect of garment construction, such as embroidery, lace-making, or pleating. This division of labor ensured the highest standards of craftsmanship and allowed the house to produce intricate, high-quality garments efficiently.

The legacy of the House of Worth lies not only in its designs but also in its transformation of the fashion industry. Worth redefined what it meant to be a designer, introducing principles that continue to shape haute couture today. His emphasis on innovation, exclusivity, and artistry marked a turning point in the history of fashion, making the House of Worth the birthplace of modern haute couture.

The Role of Fashion Magazines

Fashion magazines emerged as a powerful medium in shaping public perception and spreading the ideals of modern fashion during the late 19th century. As the industrial revolution brought literacy and leisure to the growing middle class, these publications gained widespread influence, bridging the gap between the elite world of haute couture and an expanding audience of fashion-conscious readers.

One of the earliest and most influential fashion magazines was *La Mode Illustrée*, founded in Paris in 1843. Targeted at women, it featured detailed illustrations of the latest styles, offering readers a glimpse into the world of haute couture. These images, often hand-drawn and colored, showcased garments from leading designers such as Charles Frederick Worth and his contemporaries. *La Mode Illustrée* quickly became a crucial medium for disseminating the latest trends, allowing women who couldn't travel to Paris to follow its fashion innovations.

Illustrations were the centerpiece of 19th-century fashion magazines. Before the widespread use of photography, artists were vital in translating haute couture designs into visually appealing formats. These drawings emphasized silhouette, fabric texture, and ornamentation, making it possible for readers to replicate the styles through local dressmakers. In this way, fashion magazines democratized access to high fashion, bringing elements of Parisian couture into homes across Europe and the Americas.

By the 1860s, advancements in printing technology allowed for the mass production of fashion magazines. This technological leap, combined with the growth of railroads and postal networks, ensured that publications reached a global audience. Magazines such as *Harper's Bazaar* (founded in 1867) and *The Englishwoman's Domestic Magazine* (launched in 1852) catered to an international readership, often reprinting content from Parisian publications. These magazines helped solidify Paris's reputation as the world's fashion capital, presenting its trends as aspirational ideals.

Fashion magazines were more than catalogues of styles; they also served as cultural arbiters, shaping how women thought about clothing and identity. Articles offered advice on how to dress for specific occasions, providing guidelines that reinforced societal norms. For example, advice columns instructed women on appropriate mourning attire, wedding dresses, or garments for various social functions. These articles reinforced the idea that fashion was not just about appearance but also about behavior and decorum.

During the Victorian period, fashion magazines also were influential in promoting **Victorian ideals of femininity**. They celebrated modesty, elegance, and domesticity, encouraging women to express these values through their clothing. At the same time, they offered glimpses of modernity, introducing readers to innovations in design and construction. For instance, magazines often highlighted technological advancements, such as new dyeing techniques or the use of synthetic fabrics, bridging the gap between tradition and progress.

Advertisements became a prominent feature of fashion magazines in the late 19th century. They promoted everything from sewing machines to ready-made corsets, reflecting the changing dynamics of the fashion industry. As industrialization made mass-produced goods more accessible, advertisements in fashion magazines encouraged readers to embrace modernity while still aspiring to the elegance of haute couture.

American publications like *Godey's Lady's Book* adapted the European model of fashion magazines, tailoring content to the tastes of the growing middle class in the United States. These magazines often featured patterns that readers could use to create their own versions of fashionable garments. By providing both inspiration and practical tools, they empowered women to participate in the world of fashion, even if they couldn't afford custom-made couture.

The impact of fashion magazines extended beyond the wealthy. While haute couture remained the domain of an elite few, the styles and trends featured in magazines filtered down to the middle and working classes through **ready-to-wear clothing** and local dressmakers. Magazines acted as intermediaries, translating high fashion into accessible styles that could be adapted to different budgets and social contexts.

By the late 19th century, fashion magazines began incorporating photography, marking a significant shift in how fashion was presented and consumed. Early photographs, though limited by technological constraints, offered a new level of realism, allowing readers to see how garments looked on actual models. This innovation further cemented the role of magazines as trendsetters, showcasing the artistry of haute couture while making it more relatable.

The editorial content of fashion magazines also reflected the growing influence of designers. Charles Frederick Worth, for example, was frequently featured in publications, reinforcing his status as the preeminent figure in haute couture. These profiles elevated the designer from an anonymous craftsman to a celebrated artist, shaping the public's understanding of fashion as a creative endeavor.

Fashion magazines not only chronicled the rise of haute couture but also contributed to its global reach. They fostered a sense of aspiration among readers, presenting Parisian fashion as the gold standard. This perception encouraged wealthy clients to travel to Paris to commission garments, further solidifying the city's dominance in the fashion industry.

By highlighting seasonal trends, fashion magazines introduced the concept of **fashion cycles**. Readers learned to associate certain styles with specific times of year, creating a demand for new garments as seasons changed. This practice aligned with the efforts of designers like Worth, who emphasized seasonal collections, and established a framework for the modern fashion calendar.

Fashion magazines also documented the cultural shifts of the era. As women's roles in society began to evolve in the late 19th century, magazines reflected these changes through their coverage of fashion. The increasing popularity of sportswear, for instance, mirrored the growing participation of women in outdoor activities. Similarly, articles on practical clothing for travel and work acknowledged the expanding horizons of their readers.

Ultimately, fashion magazines were instrumental in the birth of modern fashion. They served as conduits for innovation, amplifying the influence of haute couture while making it accessible to a broader audience. Through their illustrations, articles, and advertisements, these publications bridged the gap between the exclusivity of Parisian fashion and the aspirations of readers worldwide.

The Influence of the Belle Époque on Fashion

The **Belle Époque** (roughly 1871–1914) was a transformative period in the history of fashion, marked by a convergence of technological innovation, artistic experimentation, and cultural change. Rooted in the optimism and prosperity that characterized this era, fashion during the Belle Époque reflected a desire for elegance, opulence, and creative expression. It was a time when haute couture flourished, setting the stage for the birth of modern fashion.

The Belle Époque unfolded as industrialization and technological advances reshaped society. The textile industry benefited immensely from new machinery, enabling the production of high-quality fabrics at unprecedented scales. Materials like silk, velvet, and lace became more accessible, providing designers with greater variety to experiment with textures and layering. In addition, synthetic dyes allowed for an explosion of vivid colors, including deep purples, vibrant reds, and electric blues, which became hallmarks of Belle Époque fashion.

At the heart of this period was the **S-curve silhouette**, a defining feature of women's fashion. Unlike the crinoline-supported bell-shaped skirts of earlier decades, the S-curve silhouette emphasized a more fluid, feminine line. Achieved through the use of corsets that pushed the bust forward and hips back, this silhouette created a striking posture often referred to as the "Gibson Girl" look, named after the popular illustrations of Charles Dana Gibson. While these corsets were restrictive, they signaled a shift in aesthetics, focusing on curves and a sensual, hourglass shape rather than the stiffness of previous Victorian styles.

The **Gibson Girl**, as an idealized vision of the modern woman, captured the spirit of the Belle Époque. She was fashionable, confident, and socially active, embodying the era's fascination with beauty and progress. Her influence extended beyond clothing into hairstyles and attitudes, reinforcing the connection between fashion and emerging ideas about femininity and independence. This image drove demand for the tailored skirts, shirtwaists, and wide-brimmed hats that defined daywear during this time.

Evening wear during the Belle Époque epitomized extravagance. Gowns featured layers of sumptuous fabrics adorned with embroidery, beads, and appliqué. Designers like **Charles Frederick Worth** and his successors at the House of Worth catered to an elite clientele, creating custom garments that were as much works of art as they were items of clothing. These evening gowns often incorporated flowing trains and elaborate drapery, underscoring the opulence of the period. Sleeves varied in style, from puffed "leg-of-mutton" designs to slim, fitted options, reflecting the flexibility and diversity of fashion trends during this era.

The **artistic movements** of the Belle Époque deeply influenced fashion design. Art Nouveau, with its emphasis on organic forms, flowing lines, and nature-inspired motifs, found its way into the patterns and embellishments of clothing. Designers integrated floral embroidery, asymmetrical draping, and curved seams that mimicked the fluidity of Art Nouveau architecture and decorative arts. Jewelry, accessories, and even the shapes of hats were similarly inspired, blending fashion with the artistic zeitgeist of the time.

Hats were common in Belle Époque fashion. Large, elaborate designs were in vogue, often featuring ribbons, flowers, feathers, or even taxidermied birds. Milliners like **Caroline Reboux** became celebrated figures in their own right, crafting headpieces that completed the luxurious ensembles of the era. These hats were not merely accessories but statements of status and taste, often costing as much as an entire outfit.

The **rise of ready-to-wear clothing** began during this period, further shaping the fashion landscape. While haute couture dominated for the elite, the growing middle class sought more affordable options that still reflected current trends. Department stores, which proliferated during the Belle Époque, became hubs of fashion for urban consumers. Stores like Le Bon Marché in Paris offered ready-made garments alongside luxurious accessories, democratizing access to stylish clothing while still preserving the aspirational allure of haute couture.

Paris retained its status as the epicenter of fashion during the Belle Époque. Designers like **Paul Poiret**, who rose to prominence toward the end of the era, began to challenge traditional silhouettes and experiment with more relaxed, Eastern-inspired designs. Poiret introduced garments that eliminated the corset entirely, such as his famous "lampshade" tunics and draped dresses, paving the way for future innovations in modern fashion. Though not representative of the mainstream during the Belle Époque, Poiret's designs hinted at a growing interest in freedom and experimentation that would define the 20th century.

Another significant influence on Belle Époque fashion was the **theater and entertainment industry**. The rise of cabaret and operetta, along with the popularity of stars like Sarah Bernhardt, brought theatrical styles into the public eye. Costumes worn on stage often blurred the line between fantasy and fashion, inspiring eveningwear and accessories. Designers collaborated with performers to create striking looks that could be adapted for wealthy patrons attending social events, balls, or soirées.

The **social customs** of the Belle Époque also dictated fashion trends. Attire was carefully categorized by occasion, with strict expectations for daywear, afternoon dresses, and evening gowns. A woman's wardrobe reflected her social standing and ability to navigate these conventions, which required multiple outfit changes throughout the day. Tailored walking suits with high collars were popular for outings and travel, while tea gowns offered a more relaxed yet still elegant option for receiving guests at home.

Men's fashion during the Belle Époque remained more restrained but underwent subtle changes. The three-piece suit became a staple, with innovations in tailoring creating a more streamlined silhouette. Morning coats and frock coats continued to be worn for formal occasions, while sack suits gained popularity for day-to-day wear. Accessories such as pocket watches, gloves, and canes completed the refined look expected of gentlemen during this era.

Fashion during the Belle Époque was not just about aesthetics; it was intertwined with the broader cultural shifts of the time. The expansion of leisure activities, including seaside holidays, necessitated new types of clothing, such as **bathing costumes** and lighter, more practical fabrics for travel. Similarly, the popularity of cycling and other sports influenced women's fashion, leading to the creation of tailored separates and even early iterations of trousers.

Photography and the early film industry began to document Belle Époque fashion, further amplifying its impact. Portrait photography, in particular, immortalized the elaborate garments of the era, preserving them as symbols of wealth and sophistication. These images also served as a form of advertisement, showcasing the designs of leading couturiers to an audience beyond their immediate clients.

The emergence of fashion magazines during this period provided another avenue for disseminating Belle Époque styles. Publications like *La Mode Illustrée* and *Harper's Bazaar* featured detailed illustrations and articles that highlighted the latest trends, influencing readers' choices and reinforcing the importance of Paris as the global fashion leader. These magazines also had a role in shaping the consumer culture that would become central to modern fashion.

Globalization during the Belle Époque introduced new influences into European fashion. Trade with Asia and the Middle East brought exotic textiles, patterns, and design elements that were adapted into Western garments. Japanese kimonos and Chinese silk robes inspired looser silhouettes and decorative motifs, offering an alternative to the tightly structured styles of earlier decades. These cross-cultural exchanges enriched the fashion of the Belle Époque, reflecting the interconnectedness of the world during this period.

At its core, the Belle Époque was a celebration of elegance, artistry, and innovation. It was a time when fashion moved beyond practicality, embracing beauty and creativity as central to its purpose. The influence of this period on the birth of modern fashion cannot be overstated, as it laid the groundwork for the transformation of clothing into a dynamic and expressive form of cultural identity.

CHAPTER 9: THE EARLY 20TH CENTURY

The Influence of World Wars on Fashion

The two World Wars of the early 20th century reshaped fashion in profound ways. The disruptions of daily life, scarcity of materials, and shifting social roles all left their marks on how people dressed. Clothing adapted to meet the demands of wartime realities, and in the process, new trends, attitudes, and innovations emerged that would shape modern fashion.

When **World War I** broke out in 1914, the shift in clothing was immediate. With millions of men conscripted, women entered the workforce in unprecedented numbers, taking on roles that required practical attire. Long skirts with full hems gave way to shorter, more manageable styles. Hemlines rose several inches above the ankle—an enormous shift in an era when modesty had long dictated floor-length dresses. These shorter skirts allowed for freer movement, making it easier for women to work in factories, offices, and other war-related jobs.

Blouses and tailored jackets became staples of women's wardrobes during World War I. The **shirtwaist**, already popular in the Edwardian era, gained new prominence for its simplicity and versatility. Many women paired these with ankle-length skirts in darker, durable fabrics. Corsets, which had been a mainstay of women's fashion, fell out of favor. Instead, lighter, less restrictive undergarments like camisoles and simple brassieres gained popularity, marking a shift toward comfort over formality.

Military influence also crept into civilian fashion. **Trench coats**, for example, became widely adopted during and after World War I. Originally designed as part of soldiers' uniforms, these practical coats—made from water-resistant gabardine—quickly found favor among civilians. Designers like Burberry, who had created the military-style trench coat, adapted it for everyday wear, creating one of the most enduring outerwear styles in history.

Fabric rationing during World War I forced changes in garment construction. Decorative embellishments such as lace and beadwork became less common, and simpler designs took precedence. Clothing was often made from wool or cotton, as silk was redirected for military purposes, such as making parachutes. Even buttons were rationed, leading to the use of hooks, ties, or simpler fasteners in many garments. These restrictions inadvertently ushered in a more minimalist aesthetic.

When **World War II** began in 1939, the impact on fashion was even more pronounced. Wartime governments introduced strict regulations on clothing production to conserve resources. In Britain, the **Utility Clothing Scheme** mandated that garments be practical, durable, and economical in their use of fabric.

Designers were required to adhere to guidelines that limited the number of seams, pleats, and pockets. Zippers, considered more economical than buttons, became standard. These constraints led to the rise of functional, streamlined designs that emphasized utility over decoration.

The restrictions of war encouraged creativity. Designers found ways to make attractive clothing within tight limits. **Norman Hartnell**, a leading British couturier, contributed designs to the Utility Clothing Scheme, showing that even regulated garments could have style. Simple A-line skirts, tailored jackets, and dresses with modest yet elegant details became hallmarks of wartime fashion. The scheme also democratized fashion by making stylish, affordable clothing available to a wider audience.

In the United States, the **War Production Board** imposed similar restrictions on clothing through the **L-85 Regulations**, which aimed to conserve materials for the war effort. Skirts were shortened to save fabric, leading to the prevalence of knee-length styles. Women's suits, often made from wool blends, became a wardrobe essential, reflecting the influence of military uniforms. These suits were typically worn with practical shoes and hats, completing a look that balanced femininity with functionality.

Accessories gained importance during World War II as a way to add personality to otherwise simple outfits. Women used colorful scarves, bold jewelry, and statement hats to brighten their wardrobes. Red lipstick became a symbol of resilience and patriotism, encouraged by governments and cosmetic companies alike as a morale booster. It was an affordable luxury that allowed women to maintain a sense of glamour despite the hardships of war.

The war also revolutionized footwear. With leather and rubber in short supply, manufacturers turned to alternative materials. **Wedges**, made with cork or wooden soles, became popular during the 1940s. These shoes were practical yet stylish, and their popularity persisted long after the war ended. Innovations like synthetic rubber also emerged during this time, setting the stage for new developments in shoe design.

Men's fashion during the World Wars was dominated by military uniforms, but civilian styles were also affected. With many men serving in the armed forces, civilian clothing became simpler and less varied. In Britain, the government encouraged men to "Make Do and Mend," repairing and reusing existing garments rather than purchasing new ones. In the United States, mass production of military uniforms introduced standardized sizing, a practice that would later influence the ready-to-wear industry.

Post-war shortages extended the impact of the wars on fashion. In the years immediately following World War II, rationing continued in many countries, and luxury materials remained scarce. However, the end of the war also brought a desire for renewal and celebration. Designers responded by creating styles that symbolized hope and a return to normalcy.

The influence of the wars on fashion extended beyond practical considerations. Both conflicts had profound cultural effects that shaped attitudes toward clothing. During World War I, for instance, the widespread involvement of women in the workforce challenged traditional gender roles, leading to the adoption of more androgynous styles. Tailored suits, trousers, and utilitarian garments became symbols of women's independence and capabilities.

Similarly, World War II accelerated the integration of women into professional roles, further normalizing practical, work-appropriate clothing. **Trousers**, once considered inappropriate for women, became a staple during the 1940s. Women working in factories, fields, and offices embraced slacks for their practicality, and this shift laid the groundwork for trousers to become an accepted part of women's fashion in the decades to come.

The wars also changed the perception of clothing as a commodity. Before World War I, fashion had been dominated by bespoke tailoring and haute couture. However, the necessity of mass-producing uniforms during the wars created new efficiencies in manufacturing. These innovations made ready-to-wear clothing more accessible and affordable, leading to its eventual dominance in the fashion industry. Standardized sizing, developed for military purposes, became the norm for civilian clothing, streamlining production and expanding markets.

World War II, in particular, highlighted the global interconnectedness of fashion. With Paris, the traditional center of haute couture, occupied by Nazi forces, designers in other cities gained prominence. American designers, who had previously been overshadowed by their European counterparts, stepped into the spotlight. Figures like **Claire McCardell** introduced casual, practical styles that resonated with wartime sensibilities, such as her "popover" dress, which combined comfort and elegance. This marked the beginning of the United States as a major player in the global fashion industry.

The wars also spurred the development of new materials. During World War II, the need for parachutes, tents, and other military supplies led to advancements in synthetic fabrics like nylon. Nylon stockings, introduced before the war, became scarce during the conflict as the material was diverted for military use. After the war, their return to store shelves symbolized a return to peacetime luxury. These innovations paved the way for other synthetic materials like polyester, which would become staples of mid-20th-century fashion.

In occupied France during World War II, the fashion industry faced unique challenges. German authorities sought to control the output of Parisian couture houses, redirecting resources to support their war efforts. Despite these restrictions, Paris remained a symbol of resilience and creativity. Designers like **Coco Chanel** and **Lucien Lelong** navigated these difficult circumstances, with some aligning with the occupiers and others subtly resisting. Paris's fashion houses preserved their legacy even under occupation, ensuring their survival for the post-war period.

Wartime propaganda also used fashion as a tool to convey messages of unity and resilience. Governments encouraged citizens to embrace thriftiness and resourcefulness, with campaigns like Britain's "Make Do and Mend" promoting the repair and repurposing of clothing. These initiatives not only conserved resources but also reinforced a sense of collective effort. Fashion, in this context, became a reflection of broader societal values during the war.

The influence of the World Wars on fashion was as much about adaptation as it was about innovation. Necessity drove changes in materials, design, and manufacturing, while the cultural shifts caused by the wars reshaped attitudes toward clothing. The result was a period of profound transformation, where practicality and creativity came together to redefine fashion for a new era.

The Advent of Ready-to-Wear

The early 20th century marked the **advent of ready-to-wear clothing**, a revolution that fundamentally changed how people accessed fashion. This shift was driven by advancements in manufacturing, urbanization, and the growing middle class's demand for affordable, stylish clothing. Ready-to-wear garments bridged the gap between haute couture and mass production, making fashionable clothing accessible to a broader audience.

Before ready-to-wear, most clothing was either made at home, ordered from a tailor, or custom-fitted by a dressmaker. This process was labor-intensive and time-consuming, limiting access to fashionable attire. Industrialization and the rise of mechanized textile production in the late 19th century set the stage for ready-to-wear. By the early 20th century, **standardized sizing**, first developed for military uniforms during the World Wars, enabled manufacturers to produce garments in bulk that fit the average consumer reasonably well.

Department stores became central to the spread of ready-to-wear. These retail giants, such as **Sears, Roebuck and Co.** in the United States and **Selfridges** in the UK, offered racks of pre-made garments alongside luxury goods. This format transformed shopping into a public and social activity, where consumers could browse collections and try on clothes. Ready-to-wear was not limited to urban centers; catalog sales brought mass-produced clothing to rural areas, extending its reach far beyond city boundaries.

The styles of the time lent themselves to mass production. Early 20th-century silhouettes, such as shirtwaists for women and simple sack suits for men, were relatively straightforward to construct and fit. Women's day dresses, often featuring loose bodices and straight skirts, required less tailoring than earlier Victorian styles, making them easier to manufacture on a large scale. Similarly, men's suits with unstructured jackets and standard lapels became staples of the ready-to-wear market.

The rise of ready-to-wear coincided with the emergence of **sportswear** as a distinct category of fashion. As leisure activities like tennis, cycling, and swimming gained popularity, manufacturers produced practical, affordable clothing to meet these new demands. Simple designs, like tennis skirts and knit sweaters, were ideal for mass production and became widely available in department stores and catalogs.

Immigrant labor fueled the growth of the ready-to-wear industry, particularly in cities like New York, where garment factories employed thousands of workers. However, this rapid expansion came with significant challenges. Factory conditions were often harsh, with long hours, low wages, and unsafe environments. The infamous **Triangle Shirtwaist Factory fire of 1911**, which killed 146 garment workers, highlighted the dangers of the industry and led to reforms that improved labor conditions.

Ready-to-wear also intersected with technological innovation. The invention of the **electric sewing machine** sped up production, while improvements in fabric dyeing and printing allowed for vibrant, durable patterns. Synthetic fabrics like rayon emerged during this time, offering a cheaper alternative to silk and expanding options for consumers.

While ready-to-wear initially targeted middle- and working-class buyers, its influence extended to all social strata. Even high society began to incorporate off-the-rack items into their wardrobes, often blending them with bespoke pieces. This blurring of class distinctions in fashion was a hallmark of the early 20th century, as ready-to-wear democratized access to stylish clothing and reshaped how people engaged with fashion.

Flapper Fashion and the Roaring Twenties

The **Roaring Twenties** ushered in a bold, transformative era for fashion, epitomized by the **flapper**—a young, modern woman who rejected traditional norms and embraced a new, liberated identity. Flapper fashion reflected this cultural shift, characterized by shorter hemlines, looser silhouettes, and a daring embrace of self-expression. It was a dramatic departure from the structured, modest styles of earlier decades.

At the heart of flapper fashion was the rejection of the corset. Women abandoned heavily boned undergarments in favor of **step-in chemises** and **soft brassieres** that allowed for freedom of movement. This shift flattened the bust and created the boyish, androgynous silhouette associated with the era. The flapper look emphasized straight lines and a dropped waist, with dresses often hanging loosely from the shoulders. This style was practical, comfortable, and emblematic of the broader social freedoms women were beginning to enjoy.

The **shortened hemline** became one of the most iconic features of flapper fashion. By the mid-1920s, skirts that once hovered near the ankles had risen to just below the knee. This dramatic change scandalized older generations but symbolized the spirit of rebellion that defined the flapper. Shorter skirts were often paired with **flesh-colored stockings**, made possible by the development of synthetic fabrics like rayon. Women wore these stockings with rolled garters or even attached them directly to their undergarments, another departure from earlier, more restrictive attire.

Flapper dresses often featured embellishments that added movement and glamour. **Fringe, beads, and sequins** were common, designed to catch the light during dances like the Charleston or the Lindy Hop. The fluidity of these decorations mirrored the energy of the Jazz Age, as music, nightlife, and socializing became central to urban life. Evening dresses often showcased bold geometric patterns or Art Deco-inspired designs, reflecting the aesthetic trends of the time.

Accessories completed the flapper's look. **Cloche hats**, with their snug fit and narrow brim, became a signature piece, framing the short, bobbed hairstyles that were all the rage. The bob itself was revolutionary, symbolizing independence and modernity. Some women took this even further with the **Eton crop**, an ultra-short haircut that shocked more conservative observers. Hair embellishments, like jeweled headbands or feathers, added flair for evening outings.

Makeup was another hallmark of flapper style. Women in the 1920s openly embraced cosmetics, which had previously been associated with actresses or "loose" women. **Dark eyeliner, bold red lips, and rouged cheeks** became fashionable, with beauty icons like Clara Bow setting the standard. The rise of department store beauty counters and brands like Max Factor and Maybelline made makeup accessible to the masses, cementing its place in everyday life.

Flapper fashion was also heavily influenced by technological and cultural changes. The spread of **electricity** and modern manufacturing techniques allowed for more intricate beading and embroidery. Meanwhile, the invention of the **zipper** made garments easier to put on and take off, aligning with the flapper's active lifestyle. Automobiles and public transportation encouraged more practical clothing, with shorter skirts and tailored coats designed for mobility.

Economic prosperity in the post-World War I period fueled the rise of flapper fashion. For many young women, the newfound ability to earn their own income meant greater autonomy over their wardrobes. Department stores became hubs of flapper style, offering affordable dresses, accessories, and cosmetics that mirrored the latest trends. Ready-to-wear lines catered specifically to this demographic, ensuring that even working-class women could participate in the fashion revolution.

The flapper look wasn't just about style; it was a statement. It represented a rejection of Victorian ideals of femininity, which emphasized modesty and domesticity. Instead, the flapper embraced a lifestyle of freedom, fun, and exploration. Smoking, drinking, and dancing in public became symbols of this newfound independence. Fashion, in this context, was both a reflection of these changes and a catalyst for further transformation.

Flapper fashion also drew inspiration from global influences. The **Egyptian Revival**, sparked by the discovery of King Tutankhamun's tomb in 1922, introduced motifs like hieroglyphics, scarabs, and geometric patterns into clothing and accessories. Similarly, Asian influences appeared in silk kimonos and embroidered shawls, which flappers often draped over their shoulders for evening outings. These global touches added an exotic flair to the modern look.

Despite its association with urban nightlife, flapper fashion also permeated daywear. Simple, straight-cut dresses in lightweight fabrics like cotton or jersey became staples for everyday wear. These dresses often featured sailor collars, pleats, or decorative buttons, balancing practicality with style. For colder months, women wore **cocoon coats** with fur trim, combining warmth with the elegance expected of the decade.

The flapper movement wasn't without its critics. Traditionalists decried the short skirts, makeup, and nightlife culture as symbols of moral decline. Satirical cartoons and editorials mocked the flapper as frivolous or rebellious. Yet these criticisms only solidified the flapper's place in history as a symbol of change. The fashion of the Roaring Twenties represented not just a new aesthetic but a shift in values, as women asserted their right to dress, act, and live as they pleased.

The impact of flapper fashion was felt worldwide. In Europe, designers like **Coco Chanel** embraced the looser, more relaxed silhouettes that flapper fashion popularized, introducing jersey fabrics and casual elegance to haute couture. In the United States, the influence of Hollywood amplified the trend, as movie stars became style icons for millions of women. The global spread of flapper fashion underscored its significance as more than just a fleeting trend—it was a movement that redefined women's fashion for decades to come.

Art Deco and Modernist Movements

The **Art Deco** and **Modernist movements** of the early 20th century had a profound influence on fashion, shaping aesthetics, materials, and design philosophies during this transformative period. Emerging from the cultural shifts following World War I, these movements reflected a desire for innovation and a break from tradition. Fashion during this time mirrored the bold geometry and streamlined forms of Art Deco while incorporating the functional and minimalistic principles of Modernism.

Art Deco, which reached its peak in the 1920s and 1930s, was characterized by its bold, geometric designs and luxurious materials. The movement found its way into fashion through intricate embellishments, vibrant patterns, and structural silhouettes. Dresses of the era often featured angular shapes, chevrons, and zigzags, with beadwork and embroidery accentuating these motifs. The influence of Art Deco was particularly evident in evening wear, where metallic threads, sequins, and glass beads created shimmering surfaces that reflected light, enhancing the glamour of the Jazz Age.

One hallmark of Art Deco fashion was the **use of luxurious materials**. Designers incorporated fabrics like silk, satin, and velvet, as well as materials inspired by modern technology, such as cellophane threads and metallic lamé. These textiles echoed the opulence seen in Art Deco architecture and interior design. The emphasis on sleek, reflective surfaces tied fashion to the era's fascination with industry and progress, blurring the line between art and machine.

Accessories during the Art Deco period were equally striking. Jewelry designs by houses like **Cartier** and **Van Cleef & Arpels** embraced the movement's aesthetic, with pieces featuring geometric patterns, bold color contrasts, and exotic materials like onyx, jade, and coral. These designs often drew inspiration from ancient civilizations, particularly Egyptian and Aztec art, reflecting the global influences that defined Art Deco. Long, dangling earrings, stacked bracelets, and statement necklaces became essential components of the modern woman's wardrobe, complementing the simplicity of flapper-style dresses.

Art Deco also influenced footwear and millinery. Shoes featured sharp, angular heels and decorative cutouts, combining elegance with modernity. Hats adopted streamlined shapes, with cloche designs dominating the 1920s. These close-fitting styles, often embellished with Art Deco-inspired brooches or appliqués, perfectly matched the short bobbed hairstyles of the era, creating a cohesive and contemporary look.

Modernism, in contrast, emphasized function, simplicity, and the rejection of ornamentation. While Art Deco reveled in decoration, Modernism stripped away excess to focus on clean lines and utility. Influenced by movements like the **Bauhaus** and **De Stijl**, Modernist fashion reflected an architectural approach to design. Garments were created with an emphasis on structure and practicality, favoring geometric shapes and block colors over intricate patterns.

One of the key figures in Modernist fashion was **Gabrielle "Coco" Chanel**, whose minimalist designs resonated with the movement's ethos. Chanel revolutionized women's clothing by introducing simple, unadorned garments that prioritized comfort and elegance. Her use of jersey fabric, traditionally reserved for men's underwear, challenged conventional notions of luxury and femininity. The Modernist principles in her work were evident in her clean silhouettes, tailored suits, and monochromatic palettes, which provided a stark contrast to the elaborate styles of previous decades.

Modernism's focus on functionality was also reflected in the rise of **sportswear** during the early 20th century. As women became more active, designers created clothing that allowed for greater freedom of movement. Trousers, tennis skirts, and knitwear became staples of the Modernist wardrobe, emphasizing practicality without sacrificing style. The integration of zippers, pockets, and other utilitarian details further underscored the movement's commitment to design that served a purpose.

The influence of Modernism extended to evening wear, where designers experimented with asymmetry and innovative cuts. Dresses featured draped panels, sharp angles, and unconventional hemlines, reflecting the Modernist fascination with geometry and balance. These designs often relied on high-quality tailoring rather than embellishments to create visual interest, showcasing the craftsmanship that underpinned Modernist fashion.

Art Deco and Modernism intersected in their embrace of **new technologies and materials**. The early 20th century saw significant advancements in textile manufacturing, including the development of synthetic fabrics like rayon and acetate. These materials allowed designers to achieve effects that were previously impossible, such as fluid drapes and shimmering surfaces. Art Deco designers used these innovations to create glamorous, futuristic looks, while Modernists valued their practicality and affordability.

As mentioned, the global reach of these movements was another defining characteristic. Both Art Deco and Modernism were shaped by international influences, reflecting the cultural exchanges of the era. Ancient Egyptian motifs and the rise of Japanese woodblock prints and African art inspired bold, abstract patterns that aligned with the aesthetics of both movements.

Hollywood was influential in popularizing Art Deco and Modernist styles. Film stars like **Marlene Dietrich** and **Joan Crawford** embodied the glamour of the era, wearing designs that showcased the sleek lines and luxurious details of Art Deco fashion. Costume designers like **Adrian** and **Travis Banton** incorporated these aesthetics into their work, influencing how audiences around the world perceived modern style. The silver screen became a platform for experimentation, where the interplay of light and shadow highlighted the movement's geometric forms and shimmering textures.

Art Deco's emphasis on luxury and Modernism's focus on practicality found common ground in their celebration of **individualism**. Both movements challenged traditional norms and encouraged self-expression through fashion. This spirit of innovation resonated with the societal changes of the early 20th century, as women gained greater autonomy and embraced new roles in the workforce and public life. Clothing became a reflection of these shifts, blending artistry with the realities of modern living.

The streamlined aesthetics of Art Deco and Modernism also influenced **menswear**, which adopted cleaner lines and simpler silhouettes during this period. Three-piece suits became slimmer and more tailored, reflecting the efficiency and precision associated with Modernist principles. Accessories like ties and cufflinks featured geometric patterns, echoing the Art Deco style without overwhelming the overall look.

The legacy of Art Deco and Modernism in early 20th-century fashion is evident in their ability to balance innovation with timelessness. These movements introduced designs that were both forward-thinking and deeply rooted in the cultural and technological contexts of their time. By embracing geometry, functionality, and the possibilities of new materials, Art Deco and Modernism set the stage for a modern aesthetic that continues to influence fashion to this day.

CHAPTER 10: MID-CENTURY FASHION

Dior's New Look

In 1947, Christian Dior unveiled his debut collection, and with it, he transformed the world of fashion. Known as the **"New Look"**, this revolutionary style marked a dramatic departure from the austere, utilitarian clothing of World War II. It celebrated femininity, luxury, and a return to glamour in a world eager to move on from the hardships of the war. Dior's designs redefined women's fashion and reestablished Paris as the center of haute couture.

The cornerstone of Dior's New Look was the **exaggerated hourglass silhouette**. His garments featured a nipped-in waist, a fitted bodice, and full skirts that flared out dramatically from the hips. Skirts often fell to mid-calf or below, using an extravagant amount of fabric—sometimes up to 20 yards for a single gown. This excessive use of material was intentional. It symbolized abundance in stark contrast to the fabric rationing of wartime, where every inch of cloth was accounted for.

One of the most iconic pieces from the New Look collection was the **Bar Suit**, which perfectly encapsulated the essence of Dior's vision. The suit's tailored jacket featured a sharply defined waist and padded hips, creating an almost sculptural effect. It was paired with a voluminous pleated skirt that swept gracefully around the legs. The Bar Suit was an immediate sensation, and photographs of it quickly spread around the world, becoming synonymous with Dior's name.

Dior's designs were luxurious in every sense of the word. He used fine fabrics like silk, taffeta, and wool, often sourced from the best textile houses in Europe. His attention to detail extended to every aspect of construction, with couture techniques ensuring perfect tailoring and finish. The New Look required the expertise of highly skilled artisans, from seamstresses to embroiderers, who worked tirelessly to bring Dior's vision to life. This commitment to craftsmanship underscored the exclusivity of his creations.

The timing of the New Look was critical to its success. In the immediate aftermath of World War II, women's fashion had been dominated by practicality. During the war, clothing was heavily regulated by governments to conserve materials. In Britain, the **Utility Clothing Scheme** imposed strict guidelines on garment production, limiting embellishments and ensuring clothes were functional. In the United States, the **L-85 regulations** dictated skirt lengths, fabric types, and even the number of buttons on a garment. As a result, women's wardrobes were dominated by simple, tailored styles, often in somber colors.

Dior's New Look shattered these constraints. The collection was unapologetically extravagant, celebrating femininity and luxury in a way that hadn't been possible for years. For many, it represented a return to normalcy and prosperity. The world had endured years of hardship, and Dior's designs offered an optimistic vision of the future—one filled with beauty, elegance, and indulgence.

Not everyone embraced the New Look immediately. In some circles, the collection was criticized for its perceived wastefulness. The lavish use of fabric sparked protests, particularly in countries still recovering from wartime shortages. In Britain, where rationing continued into the early 1950s, some women found Dior's designs impractical and unattainable. Protesters held signs that read, "We abhor dresses to the floor!" echoing frustrations over the perceived extravagance of the full skirts.

Despite the criticism, the New Look resonated with those who could afford it. Wealthy women from Europe and the United States flocked to Dior's Paris atelier, eager to embrace his vision. Celebrities and socialites wore his creations, further cementing the New Look as a symbol of status and style. Dior's clientele included Hollywood stars like Marlene Dietrich and Grace Kelly, whose public appearances in his gowns brought global attention to the brand.

Dior's influence extended beyond couture. The New Look filtered into mainstream fashion through ready-to-wear adaptations, as manufacturers rushed to replicate the hourglass silhouette. Department stores stocked dresses with cinched waists and full skirts, offering middle-class women the opportunity to emulate Dior's style. Home sewing patterns, which became increasingly popular during this period, featured designs inspired by the New Look, allowing women to recreate the silhouette on their own.

The New Look also revived interest in accessories. Dior's ensembles were meticulously styled with gloves, hats, and shoes that completed the polished, ladylike aesthetic. Accessories had been largely overlooked during the war years, but under Dior's influence, they became essential elements of an outfit. Gloves in particular gained renewed importance, with styles ranging from wrist-length designs for daytime to opera-length gloves for evening wear.

Dior's vision for femininity extended to the underpinnings of his garments. The exaggerated silhouette of the New Look relied on structured undergarments to achieve its shape. Corsets, long abandoned by mainstream fashion, made a return, albeit in a softer, more flexible form. These garments, often referred to as **waspies** or **waist cinchers**, emphasized the hourglass figure by tightly constricting the waist. Beneath the voluminous skirts, petticoats added volume, while carefully placed padding enhanced the bust and hips.

The New Look wasn't just about fashion; it was also a statement about the changing role of women in society. The post-war years were a period of transition, as women who had worked in factories and offices during the war returned to domestic roles. The New Look, with its emphasis on elegance and femininity, aligned with traditional ideas about women's place in the home. However, it also empowered women by giving them a sense of glamour and confidence. For many, wearing Dior was an act of self-expression, a way to reclaim beauty and sophistication after years of sacrifice.

Dior's success revitalized the French fashion industry, which had struggled during the war. Paris had long been considered the epicenter of couture, but the Nazi occupation had disrupted its dominance. Many designers fled the city, and others were forced to operate under strict restrictions. Dior's New Look marked a triumphant return to form for Parisian fashion, reestablishing the city's reputation as the global capital of style.

Dior's legacy extended far beyond the initial impact of the New Look. His success paved the way for a new generation of designers, including his protégé, Yves Saint Laurent, who would later revolutionize fashion in his own right. The New Look also set the stage for the mid-century emphasis on couture, with designers like Balenciaga, Givenchy, and Chanel building on Dior's foundation to create their own visions of elegance.

By the early 1950s, the New Look had evolved into a dominant trend, influencing nearly every aspect of women's fashion. Even casualwear adopted elements of the silhouette, with blouses and skirts designed to emphasize the waist. The popularity of the style underscored the enduring appeal of Dior's vision, which celebrated beauty and craftsmanship in a way that resonated deeply with women of the time.

Christian Dior's New Look remains one of the most iconic moments in fashion history. It was more than just a collection; it was a cultural reset that redefined what women's clothing could be. Through its elegance, extravagance, and attention to detail, the New Look captured the spirit of an era and left an indelible mark on the world of fashion.

Post-War Innovation

The aftermath of World War II saw a surge of innovation in fashion as the industry responded to changing social dynamics, technological advances, and renewed demand for creativity. After years of austerity and rationing, the late 1940s and 1950s marked a period of experimentation and progress, with designers and manufacturers introducing new techniques, materials, and designs that defined mid-century fashion.

One of the most significant developments during this period was the **introduction of synthetic fabrics**. Materials like nylon, rayon, and acetate, which had been developed or refined during the war for military purposes, found their way into civilian fashion. Nylon stockings, for example, returned to the market after years of being unavailable, quickly becoming a symbol of post-war luxury and femininity. Synthetic fabrics allowed for more affordable, durable clothing that could be mass-produced, catering to the growing middle class.

Advances in textile technology also gave rise to **wash-and-wear fabrics**, which revolutionized everyday clothing. These materials were easier to clean and required less maintenance than traditional fabrics like cotton or wool, appealing to busy post-war households. The introduction of **polyester** in the 1950s further enhanced the convenience of fashion, with its wrinkle-resistant properties and ability to hold bright colors. These innovations aligned with the era's emphasis on efficiency and modern living.

The fashion industry also embraced **new construction techniques**, making garments more versatile and accessible. The widespread use of zippers replaced buttons and hooks in many designs, simplifying closures and allowing for sleeker silhouettes. Advances in garment shaping, such as darting and pleating, enabled designers to create more precise fits without relying on heavily structured undergarments. For men's fashion, improvements in tailoring techniques brought sharper, cleaner lines to suits, enhancing their appeal for a modern audience.

Post-war innovation extended to **color and pattern**. Advances in chemical dyeing allowed for brighter, more vibrant colors, which were celebrated in both high fashion and ready-to-wear. Patterns like polka dots, gingham, and atomic-inspired motifs reflected the optimism and fascination with modernity that characterized the era. These bold designs were especially popular in casualwear, which saw a boom as leisure activities became an integral part of mid-century life.

The rise of **ready-to-wear fashion** was another transformative innovation. While haute couture remained a powerful force in the fashion world, the demand for affordable, accessible clothing led to an explosion of ready-to-wear lines. Brands like Dior and Balenciaga introduced secondary lines to reach a broader audience, while department stores stocked mass-produced versions of designer trends. Advances in sizing standardization and mass production enabled these garments to be produced efficiently, ensuring consistent quality.

Fashion also responded to changing social norms with more **functional and practical designs**. Women's roles during the war had expanded to include work outside the home, and although many returned to domestic life, the influence of these experiences lingered. Pants became a staple of women's wardrobes, reflecting the practicality and independence they had embraced during the war. Separates, such as mix-and-match blouses and skirts, gained popularity, offering women flexibility in their daily attire.

In men's fashion, post-war innovation brought subtle but significant changes. The **Ivy League look**, characterized by slim-cut suits, button-down shirts, and loafers, emerged as a dominant trend. This preppy style reflected the post-war focus on education and upward mobility, becoming a symbol of success and modernity. Innovations in suit construction, such as lightweight fabrics and unlined jackets, made men's clothing more comfortable and adaptable to a range of occasions.

The 1950s also saw a shift in the marketing and distribution of fashion. **Television advertising** emerged, showcasing the latest styles to a mass audience. Brands and department stores capitalized on this new medium, creating campaigns that emphasized the glamour and convenience of modern fashion. Mail-order catalogs, which had been popular in earlier decades, continued to thrive, bringing affordable clothing to rural and suburban areas.

Post-war innovation wasn't confined to high fashion; it also transformed **youth culture**. Teenagers, a newly recognized demographic, embraced trends like denim jeans, leather jackets, and poodle skirts, creating a distinct style that set them apart from their parents. These youthful fashions often drew inspiration from music and film, underscoring the growing influence of popular culture on fashion.

The Role of Hollywood in Fashion

Hollywood was a driving force in mid-century fashion, shaping trends and inspiring consumers around the world. The Golden Age of cinema, which peaked in the 1940s and 1950s, saw movie stars emerge as powerful style icons. Audiences idolized these actors and actresses, often imitating their on-screen looks in their everyday lives. Designers and costume departments were influential in this phenomenon, creating memorable wardrobes that blurred the line between fiction and reality.

One of the most influential figures in Hollywood fashion was **Edith Head**, a legendary costume designer who worked on hundreds of films during her career. Head's designs were tailored to each star's persona, enhancing their on-screen characters while setting trends off-screen. Her collaborations with actresses like Grace Kelly, Audrey Hepburn, and Elizabeth Taylor brought timeless looks to the silver screen. For example, Kelly's elegant wardrobe in *Rear Window* (1954) featured classic silhouettes that inspired countless women to adopt similar styles.

Hollywood's influence extended beyond women's fashion. Actors like **Cary Grant** and **James Dean** became style icons for men, embodying the polished sophistication or rebellious edge that audiences aspired to emulate. Grant's impeccably tailored suits in films like *North by Northwest* (1959) exemplified mid-century elegance, while Dean's casual ensemble of a leather jacket, white T-shirt, and jeans in *Rebel Without a Cause* (1955) defined youth culture for a generation.

The relationship between Hollywood and high fashion grew stronger during this period. Designers like **Christian Dior**, **Balenciaga**, and **Hubert de Givenchy** created custom pieces for films, further solidifying their status as arbiters of style. Givenchy's collaboration with Audrey Hepburn was particularly significant. Hepburn's black sheath dress in *Breakfast at Tiffany's* (1961), designed by Givenchy, became one of the most iconic garments in cinematic history, symbolizing timeless elegance and the enduring power of simplicity.

Hollywood's impact on fashion wasn't limited to couture. Costume designers often worked with ready-to-wear brands to create affordable versions of movie wardrobes, making it easier for consumers to adopt the styles they saw on screen. This practice, known as **film-inspired fashion**, became a lucrative industry, with retailers marketing clothing as "as seen in" or "inspired by" popular films.

The rise of Technicolor in the 1940s and 1950s amplified Hollywood's influence on fashion. Vibrant colors on screen inspired bold choices in clothing, from bright evening gowns to patterned daywear. Films like *Gentlemen Prefer Blondes* (1953) showcased Marilyn Monroe and Jane Russell in striking, jewel-toned costumes that encouraged women to experiment with color in their own wardrobes. The medium of film brought fashion to life in a way that photographs and illustrations could not, making it more tangible and aspirational.

Hollywood also shaped the marketing of fashion through its use of glamour and escapism. Studios carefully crafted the public personas of their stars, ensuring they always looked flawless in public appearances and promotional materials. Actresses like Rita Hayworth and Lauren Bacall became synonymous with sophistication, their red carpet looks setting trends that would dominate magazines and department stores. These images reinforced the idea that fashion was not just about clothing but about creating a lifestyle.

The relationship between Hollywood and fashion extended to hairstyles and makeup. Stars like Veronica Lake, with her iconic peek-a-boo waves, and Elizabeth Taylor, known for her dramatic eyeliner, influenced beauty trends as much as clothing. Women sought to replicate these looks, often purchasing products endorsed by their favorite stars. The burgeoning cosmetics industry capitalized on this connection, with brands launching lines tied to Hollywood glamour.

Internationally, Hollywood served as an ambassador for American style. European audiences, still recovering from World War II, looked to the United States for inspiration. Films exported American ideals of beauty and fashion, often influencing local trends. At the same time, Hollywood drew inspiration from global fashion, incorporating elements like French couture and Italian tailoring into its productions.

By the 1950s, Hollywood's influence had expanded to include youth fashion. Movies like *Blackboard Jungle* (1955) and *Rebel Without a Cause* popularized the edgy, rebellious styles of teenagers, including denim jeans, leather jackets, and sneakers. These looks were closely tied to the rise of rock and roll, further cementing the connection between film, music, and fashion.

Hollywood's role in mid-century fashion was multifaceted. It wasn't just a trendsetter but a bridge between haute couture and mass-market accessibility. Through the costumes worn on screen and the public personas of its stars, Hollywood defined what it meant to be stylish in the mid-20th century, leaving a mark on global fashion.

The Impact of Global Events on Design Trends

The mid-20th century was a period of rapid transformation, and global events were influential in shaping design trends during this time. Political, economic, and cultural shifts influenced fashion in profound ways, leading to new silhouettes, materials, and concepts of style. Designers responded to the changing world by creating garments that reflected the optimism, challenges, and innovations of the era.

The **Cold War** profoundly influenced mid-century fashion, fostering a climate of competition between the United States and the Soviet Union. This rivalry extended beyond politics and technology into culture and style. The United States, eager to project its values of freedom and prosperity, promoted consumer culture, including fashion, as a symbol of democracy. American designers like **Claire McCardell** and **Norman Norell** emphasized functional, modern clothing that reflected the ideals of individualism and practicality. Ready-to-wear sportswear became a hallmark of American fashion, contrasting with the rigid, uniform-like styles often associated with the Soviet bloc.

During the Cold War, the Space Race also inspired futuristic design trends. The launch of Sputnik in 1957 marked a turning point, as designers began incorporating space-age elements into their collections. Shiny, metallic fabrics, geometric shapes, and sleek, minimalist lines echoed the aesthetics of rockets and spacecraft. Accessories like **bubble-shaped helmets** and oversized sunglasses, reminiscent of astronaut gear, became popular in the late 1950s and early 1960s, previewing the eventual rise of space-age fashion.

The rebuilding of Europe after **World War II** had a direct impact on mid-century fashion. The Marshall Plan, which provided economic aid to war-torn countries, revitalized industries, including textiles and garment production. In France, the revival of haute couture under designers like **Christian Dior** and **Pierre Balmain** symbolized a return to elegance and luxury. Dior's New Look, introduced in 1947, continued to dominate into the early 1950s, representing a rejection of wartime austerity in favor of extravagance and femininity.

Italy experienced a similar renaissance during this period. With the help of American funding and the entrepreneurial spirit of Italian designers, the country established itself as a leader in ready-to-wear fashion. Designers like **Salvatore Ferragamo** and **Emilio Pucci** gained international acclaim for their innovative use of color and materials. The post-war rebuilding efforts also gave rise to Italian fashion cities like Florence and Milan, which emerged as major style hubs.

The **Korean War** (1950–1953) indirectly influenced fashion by sustaining the demand for military-inspired clothing. This trend, which had begun during World War II, persisted as designers continued to incorporate elements like structured jackets, epaulets, and utility pockets into their collections. Camouflage patterns began appearing in casual wear, reflecting the enduring presence of military aesthetics in civilian fashion.

The rise of the **civil rights movement** in the United States during the 1950s also left its mark on fashion. The growing visibility of African American culture brought influences from jazz, soul, and rhythm and blues into mainstream style. Young people, particularly in urban areas, adopted slim-fitting suits, bold prints, and polished accessories inspired by the music and performers of the time. The zoot suit, popularized earlier in the century, made a comeback among certain subcultures, symbolizing defiance and individuality.

Decolonization movements across Africa and Asia during the mid-century introduced global influences into Western fashion. As former colonies gained independence, designers and consumers became increasingly interested in non-Western textiles, patterns, and techniques. African prints, Asian silks, and Indian embroidery began appearing in high fashion, reflecting a growing appreciation for cultural diversity. French designer **Yves Saint Laurent**, for example, drew inspiration from Moroccan culture, incorporating bold colors and patterns into his work.

The **post-war baby boom** created a new focus on family-oriented lifestyles, which was reflected in fashion trends. Suburbanization and the rise of the middle class emphasized practicality and affordability, leading to the popularity of casual clothing. Women's fashion included tailored shirtwaist dresses and house dresses, which combined style with functionality. For men, the growing prevalence of white-collar jobs shifted fashion toward business attire, with gray flannel suits becoming a symbol of corporate culture.

The economic prosperity of the 1950s also fueled the rise of **youth culture** as a distinct demographic. Teenagers, benefiting from increased spending power, became trendsetters in their own right. Denim jeans, leather jackets, and sneakers gained popularity among young people, particularly those influenced by rock and roll music. Movies like *Rebel Without a Cause* (1955) and *Blackboard Jungle* (1955) highlighted these styles, reinforcing their association with rebellion and individuality.

Technological advancements during the mid-century further influenced fashion design. Innovations in synthetic fabrics like polyester, acrylic, and spandex transformed the industry by making clothing more affordable, durable, and versatile. Wash-and-wear garments, which required minimal maintenance, became staples of mid-century wardrobes, aligning with the era's focus on convenience and efficiency. These fabrics also allowed designers to experiment with new textures and finishes, such as glossy, plastic-like surfaces that complemented the futuristic aesthetics of the time.

The widespread availability of **television** during the 1950s brought fashion into people's homes like never before. Viewers were exposed to the styles of celebrities, news anchors, and even fictional characters, influencing their own wardrobes.

Television advertising also introduced audiences to new brands and trends, reinforcing the connection between consumer culture and mid-century fashion. Shows like *I Love Lucy* and *The Ed Sullivan Show* served as platforms for showcasing contemporary styles, bridging the gap between high fashion and everyday wear.

International trade agreements during the mid-century facilitated the globalization of fashion. The increased flow of goods and materials across borders allowed for greater collaboration between countries. For example, Japanese textiles gained popularity in the West, particularly silk and cotton fabrics featuring intricate prints. These materials were used in both haute couture and ready-to-wear collections, reflecting a blend of Eastern and Western influences.

Political events such as the **Red Scare** and McCarthyism shaped the cultural climate of the mid-century, indirectly affecting fashion. The era's conservative social norms encouraged modesty and conformity in clothing, particularly in the United States. Women's styles emphasized a ladylike aesthetic, with structured dresses, gloves, and pearls becoming symbols of propriety. Men's fashion adhered to similarly rigid standards, with suits and ties dominating professional attire.

The **global fascination with cinema and Hollywood glamour** during the mid-century reinforced the idea of fashion as a form of aspiration. Stars like Audrey Hepburn, Marilyn Monroe, and Grace Kelly influenced trends not only in the United States but around the world. European audiences, in particular, admired the polished elegance of American film stars, while American consumers looked to Paris for the latest couture designs. This cultural exchange between Hollywood and European fashion houses underscored the interconnectedness of mid-century design trends.

The environmental impact of global events, such as increased industrialization and urbanization, also influenced mid-century fashion. As cities expanded and pollution became a growing concern, designers began exploring more sustainable materials and production methods. While this movement was still in its infancy, it reflected an awareness of the broader consequences of industrial progress on fashion and society.

Throughout the mid-20th century, global events shaped not only what people wore but also how they thought about fashion. Designers and consumers alike responded to the changing world, creating a dynamic, interconnected fashion landscape that reflected the complexities of the era.

CHAPTER 11: THE COUNTERCULTURE SIXTIES

The Rise of Youth Culture

The 1960s marked a seismic shift in fashion, driven by the **rise of youth culture**. For the first time in history, young people became the dominant force in shaping trends, rejecting the conservative styles of their parents and embracing bold, expressive looks that reflected their desire for individuality and change. The youth of the sixties did not just follow fashion—they defined it, transforming the industry and creating a lasting cultural impact.

This transformation was fueled by **demographics and economics**. The post-war baby boom produced a generation of teenagers and young adults by the 1960s who had both disposable income and the desire to spend it. These young consumers were no longer content to dress like their parents; they sought styles that matched their vibrant, rebellious spirit. Designers and retailers quickly recognized the market potential, and fashion began catering directly to this new, influential audience.

London emerged as the epicenter of youth culture, earning its nickname, **"Swinging London."** The city became a hub for innovative fashion, music, and art, with Carnaby Street and King's Road at the heart of the scene. Boutiques like **Mary Quant's Bazaar** and **Biba** redefined retail, offering clothing that was affordable, modern, and perfectly suited to the youth market. These shops became gathering places for the style-conscious, creating a sense of community around fashion.

Mary Quant was a pivotal figure in the rise of youth culture fashion. She popularized the **miniskirt**, a garment that came to symbolize freedom and rebellion. Hemlines rose dramatically in the sixties, shocking older generations but delighting young women who embraced the skirt's playful and liberating style. Quant designed clothes that were youthful and fun, using bright colors, geometric patterns, and unconventional materials like PVC. Her designs were simple but bold, reflecting the energetic spirit of the decade.

The rise of the **mod subculture** in Britain was another major influence on youth fashion. Mods favored sleek, tailored clothing, often inspired by Italian styles. For men, this meant sharp suits, narrow ties, and polished loafers. Women adopted slim-fitting shift dresses, often paired with white boots and bold eyeliner. The mod look was clean and modern, a stark contrast to the conservative styles of the 1950s. Music and fashion were tightly intertwined in this movement, with bands like The Who and The Kinks epitomizing mod style.

In the United States, youth culture took a slightly different form, influenced by the civil rights movement, the anti-war movement, and the growing counterculture.

College students and young activists began rejecting mainstream fashion, opting for more casual, unstructured styles. Denim jeans, once associated with manual labor, became a symbol of rebellion and solidarity. Paired with T-shirts or flannel shirts, jeans reflected the practical, anti-establishment ethos of the sixties youth.

The **hippie movement**, which emerged in the mid-1960s, brought an entirely new aesthetic to youth fashion. Inspired by Eastern philosophies, nature, and communal living, hippie style rejected materialism and embraced handmade, secondhand, and ethnic clothing. Young people wore loose, flowing garments, often adorned with embroidery, fringe, or tie-dye patterns. Accessories like beaded necklaces, headbands, and sandals completed the look, emphasizing individuality and a connection to the earth.

Hippie fashion also celebrated **cultural diversity**, incorporating elements from around the world. Indian fabrics, African prints, and Native American patterns were all embraced by the movement, reflecting a broader rejection of Western consumerism. This global perspective influenced high fashion as well, with designers like Yves Saint Laurent and Emilio Pucci drawing inspiration from non-Western traditions in their collections.

Youth culture in the sixties was heavily influenced by **music**, which became both a soundtrack and a visual guide for the decade's fashion. Bands like The Beatles, The Rolling Stones, and The Doors set trends through their stage outfits and album covers. Psychedelic rock brought a kaleidoscope of patterns and colors to the forefront, inspiring everything from clothing to poster art. Woodstock in 1969 became a defining moment, showcasing the hippie aesthetic to the world and solidifying its place in history.

The rise of **unisex fashion** was another important development. Traditional gender distinctions in clothing began to blur as young people embraced styles that could be worn by anyone. Bell-bottom jeans, tunic tops, and leather jackets became staples for both men and women, challenging societal norms about masculinity and femininity. This shift reflected broader cultural changes, as the sixties youth questioned and dismantled traditional gender roles.

The rise of **affordable fashion** was instrumental in the youth culture's impact. Retailers like **Woolworths** and **JC Penney** began offering stylish clothing at prices that young people could afford, democratizing access to fashion. Synthetic fabrics like polyester and acrylic allowed manufacturers to produce trendy garments quickly and cheaply, ensuring that even working-class teenagers could participate in the latest trends. Disposable fashion, a concept that emerged in the sixties, reflected the fast-paced, ever-changing nature of youth culture.

Designers who once catered exclusively to elite clientele began embracing youth-oriented styles. André Courrèges, for example, incorporated space-age elements into his collections, creating clean, futuristic designs that resonated with the sixties' fascination with progress and technology. Pierre Cardin also embraced modernity, with bold, avant-garde pieces that challenged traditional ideas of luxury. These designers saw the youth market as a source of inspiration and innovation, blurring the lines between high fashion and street style.

The youth culture of the sixties also emphasized **individual expression**, rejecting conformity and embracing personal style. This philosophy gave rise to a mix-and-match approach to fashion, where young people combined elements from various trends and subcultures to create their own unique looks. Vintage clothing gained popularity, as did thrift shopping, allowing teenagers to experiment with style without breaking the bank. This DIY attitude toward fashion was a precursor to later trends like punk and grunge.

Advertising and media amplified the influence of youth culture. Magazines like *Seventeen* and *Honey* featured young models wearing the latest styles, providing a visual roadmap for teenagers seeking inspiration. Television shows like *Ready Steady Go!* in the UK and *The Ed Sullivan Show* in the US showcased performers in modern fashions, further spreading trends across the globe. The widespread availability of glossy imagery made fashion more accessible and aspirational than ever before.

The political climate of the sixties also shaped youth fashion. The civil rights movement brought Afrocentric styles into the mainstream, with young Black Americans wearing dashikis, headwraps, and natural hairstyles as symbols of pride and cultural identity. This embrace of heritage and individuality resonated with the broader youth culture, reinforcing the idea that fashion could be a form of protest and self-expression.

Environmentalism began to influence youth fashion toward the end of the decade. As awareness of pollution and resource depletion grew, young people started questioning the ethics of mass production and consumerism. This concern gave rise to the early sustainability movement, with some embracing handmade or recycled clothing as an alternative to the throwaway culture of the time.

Overall, the decade's embrace of freedom, individuality, and rebellion created a fashion landscape that was dynamic, diverse, and endlessly creative, setting the stage for the styles of the 1970s and beyond.

Mod Fashion and Mary Quant

Mod fashion emerged in the early 1960s as part of a larger youth-driven subculture that celebrated sleek design, vibrant colors, and individuality. Short for "modernist," the **mod movement** originated in London and quickly spread internationally, influencing fashion, music, and lifestyle. It was a stark departure from the conservative styles of the previous decade, embracing clean lines, bold patterns, and a futuristic aesthetic. At the forefront of this revolution was **Mary Quant**, a designer who became synonymous with mod fashion and youth culture.

Quant's designs embodied the energy and optimism of the era. Her boutique, **Bazaar**, located on King's Road in London, became a hub for young people seeking stylish yet affordable clothing. Quant believed fashion should be fun, accessible, and reflective of the times. She famously stated, "Good taste is death. Vulgarity is life," emphasizing her commitment to experimentation and rebellion against traditional fashion norms.

The **miniskirt** was Quant's most iconic contribution to mod fashion. Although its invention is debated, Quant popularized the miniskirt and made it a defining garment of the sixties. The hemline, which rose well above the knee, was both a practical choice for the active lifestyles of young women and a bold statement of liberation. Quant named the skirt after her favorite car, the Mini Cooper, further cementing its association with the mod movement. Paired with tights in vibrant colors or bold patterns, the miniskirt became a symbol of youthful exuberance and independence.

Mod fashion was defined by its love of **geometric shapes and striking contrasts**. Dresses often featured A-line silhouettes, sharp collars, and eye-catching patterns like checks, stripes, and polka dots. The palette was playful and bold, with black and white often used as a base for bright pops of primary colors. Quant and other designers embraced new materials like PVC, using them to create shiny, futuristic garments that captured the era's fascination with technology and progress.

Accessories were essential to completing the mod look. **Go-go boots**, often knee-high and made of white patent leather, became a staple, adding a sleek, space-age feel to outfits. Chunky plastic jewelry, oversized sunglasses, and cloche hats further emphasized the modern aesthetic. Hairstyles were equally important, with many women adopting sharp, angular cuts like the five-point bob popularized by hairdresser **Vidal Sassoon**.

Men's mod fashion was equally distinctive, emphasizing tailored, clean-cut designs influenced by Italian and French styles. Slim-cut suits, often in mohair or lightweight wool, featured narrow lapels and were worn with skinny ties or turtlenecks. Mods also embraced bold colors and patterns in their shirts and jackets, challenging traditional notions of masculinity in fashion. Footwear included pointed leather shoes and Chelsea boots, which completed the polished, sophisticated look.

Music was central to the mod subculture and its fashion. Bands like **The Who, The Kinks**, and **The Small Faces** epitomized mod style, both in their sound and their wardrobe. The sharp suits and vibrant stage outfits worn by these musicians influenced fans and reinforced the connection between mod fashion and the music scene. Carnaby Street became the epicenter of this convergence, with boutiques selling clothing inspired by or directly tied to mod icons.

Mod fashion's influence extended far beyond Britain. In the United States, the mod look gained popularity among teenagers and young adults, thanks in part to British Invasion bands like **The Beatles** and **The Rolling Stones**. American designers adapted the style for the mass market, incorporating elements like A-line dresses and slim-cut trousers into ready-to-wear collections. The mod aesthetic also found its way into advertising, where its bold colors and graphic patterns were used to target younger consumers.

The Influence of Music and Pop Art

Music and pop art were two of the most significant cultural forces of the 1960s, and both profoundly influenced the fashion of the era. These art forms resonated with the counterculture spirit, emphasizing creativity, rebellion, and a break from traditional norms. The vibrant interplay between music, visual art, and fashion gave the sixties its distinctive look and energy.

The British Invasion, led by bands like **The Beatles**, **The Rolling Stones**, and **The Who**, had a direct impact on sixties fashion. These groups not only defined the sound of the decade but also set trends with their clothing. Early in the decade, The Beatles popularized mod-inspired suits with narrow lapels and drainpipe trousers, setting the tone for a clean, polished aesthetic. As their style evolved, they embraced more experimental looks, such as colorful military jackets and psychedelic patterns, reflecting the broader shift in youth culture.

Rock music's growing influence on fashion extended to accessories and hairstyles. Men grew their hair longer, rejecting the short cuts of previous generations, while women adopted bangs and shaggy styles inspired by musicians like Marianne Faithfull and Patti Boyd. Leather jackets, fringe, and denim—worn by artists like Bob Dylan and Janis Joplin—became staples of counterculture fashion, symbolizing a rebellious, free-spirited attitude.

The **psychedelic movement**, driven by bands like **The Grateful Dead** and **Jimi Hendrix**, brought an explosion of color and pattern to sixties fashion. Inspired by hallucinogenic experiences and Eastern philosophies, this aesthetic embraced swirling, kaleidoscopic designs and vivid hues. Tie-dye shirts, paisley prints, and flowing garments became hallmarks of the look, capturing the spirit of experimentation and self-expression.

Pop art, pioneered by artists like **Andy Warhol**, **Roy Lichtenstein**, and **Peter Blake**, had an equally transformative effect on sixties fashion. The movement's use of bold graphics, bright colors, and mass-culture imagery resonated with designers who sought to challenge traditional ideas of art and beauty. Warhol's iconic prints of Campbell's soup cans and Marilyn Monroe, for example, inspired clothing and accessories that blurred the line between high art and commercial design.

The influence of pop art was particularly evident in the work of designers like **Paco Rabanne**, **Pierre Cardin**, and **André Courrèges**, who embraced the visual language of the movement in their collections. Rabanne used unconventional materials like metal and plastic to create garments that looked more like sculptures than clothing, while Cardin's space-age designs featured bold, geometric shapes reminiscent of Lichtenstein's comic book-inspired art. These avant-garde pieces pushed the boundaries of fashion, aligning perfectly with the counterculture ethos of breaking from tradition.

Pop art also influenced everyday fashion through prints and patterns. Dresses and blouses featuring bold, graphic motifs—such as oversized polka dots, stripes, or cartoon-inspired imagery—became popular among young people. The movement's playful, irreverent spirit encouraged wearers to experiment with their looks, rejecting the idea that fashion had to be serious or restrained.

Music festivals like **Woodstock** in 1969 showcased the relationship between music, art, and fashion, creating a visual representation of the counterculture. Attendees wore a mix of hippie-inspired styles, including tie-dye, fringe, and ethnic prints, reflecting the free-spirited, communal ethos of the festival. Bands performing at Woodstock further reinforced these trends, with their clothing embodying the same sense of individuality and rebellion.

The rise of album art as a medium for self-expression also influenced sixties fashion. Record covers became canvases for bold, artistic statements, with designers and musicians collaborating to create visuals that complemented the music. The Beatles' *Sgt. Pepper's Lonely Hearts Club Band* cover, designed by Peter Blake, featured a vibrant collage of cultural icons that mirrored the eclecticism of the band's music. Fans often sought to emulate these styles, creating a feedback loop between music, art, and fashion.

Television and magazines amplified the influence of music and pop art on fashion, broadcasting images of performers and their fans to a global audience. Shows like *Top of the Pops* and magazines like *Rolling Stone* highlighted the latest trends, ensuring that the aesthetics of the counterculture reached even those who weren't directly part of it. This exposure helped cement the sixties' reputation as a decade of vibrant creativity and cultural cross-pollination.

CHAPTER 12: THE 1970S: INDIVIDUALISM AND EXPRESSION

Hippie Style and Counterculture

The **hippie style** of the 1970s was born out of the counterculture movement that began in the previous decade but reached its zenith as the new decade unfolded. Rooted in values of peace, freedom, and rejection of mainstream materialism, hippie fashion became a visual statement of individuality and rebellion. It embraced natural materials, handcrafted items, and vibrant patterns, reflecting both an anti-establishment ethos and a celebration of global influences.

One of the most defining elements of hippie style was its **loose, flowing silhouettes**, which prioritized comfort and freedom of movement. Women wore maxi dresses, peasant blouses, and kaftans, often adorned with embroidery or ethnic patterns. Men embraced wide-legged trousers, tunics, and unstructured jackets, breaking away from the tailored looks of previous generations. These relaxed styles aligned with the counterculture's rejection of formality and societal norms.

Denim became a wardrobe staple for both men and women, symbolizing durability and egalitarianism. Jeans, often flared or bell-bottomed, were worn by almost everyone in the counterculture, sometimes customized with patches, embroidery, or painted designs. This personalization of clothing reflected the era's emphasis on self-expression. Distressed denim gained popularity, with rips and frayed hems celebrated as authentic and unpretentious, a sharp contrast to the polished looks of the mainstream.

Hippie fashion was heavily influenced by **non-Western cultures**, particularly those from Asia, Africa, and the Middle East. Indian textiles like paisley and batik prints were widely adopted, often used in scarves, skirts, and blouses. Afghan coats, made from sheepskin and embroidered with intricate patterns, became iconic pieces of the era. These global influences reflected the counterculture's fascination with Eastern philosophies, spirituality, and communal living.

Tie-dye, another hallmark of hippie style, was both a practical and symbolic choice. Easily created at home, tie-dye shirts, dresses, and bandanas allowed wearers to craft unique pieces that stood out from mass-produced clothing. The swirling, colorful patterns embodied the psychedelic experiences associated with the era, particularly the influence of hallucinogenic drugs on art and fashion. Tie-dye's vibrant chaos was a visual representation of freedom and creativity.

Accessories completed the hippie look and carried symbolic meanings. **Beaded necklaces**, often handmade, were worn in layers, while leather or woven bracelets adorned wrists. Headbands, often tied across the forehead, were a nod to Native American styles and reflected the counterculture's idealized connection to nature and indigenous traditions. Feathered earrings and fringed bags added to the bohemian aesthetic, emphasizing texture and natural materials.

Fringe became a key feature in hippie outerwear, particularly on suede jackets and vests. Inspired by Native American designs, fringe added movement and visual interest while connecting wearers to the natural world. It was also a subtle rejection of the clean, industrial aesthetics of mainstream fashion. Many hippie jackets were vintage or thrifted, reflecting the counterculture's emphasis on recycling and rejecting consumerism.

Footwear was equally casual and practical. Sandals, particularly leather ones like **Birkenstocks**, were popular for their comfort and association with a natural, earthy lifestyle. Moccasins, also inspired by Native American designs, became common, as did bare feet at gatherings like outdoor concerts and festivals. This approach to footwear further underscored the rejection of societal expectations for polished, formal appearances.

The rise of **handcrafted clothing and accessories** was a defining feature of hippie fashion. People often made their own garments or bought from small artisans, rejecting the conformity of mass production. Crochet and macramé became popular techniques for creating tops, bags, and even swimwear. This DIY ethos aligned with the counterculture's values of self-reliance and creativity.

Hippie style was also deeply tied to the **music festivals** of the era, particularly Woodstock in 1969 and later events in the 1970s. These gatherings became showcases for the fashion of the movement, as attendees wore flowing skirts, floral crowns, and layered jewelry. Festivals like these amplified the visibility of hippie fashion, solidifying its place in cultural history.

Florals were another recurring motif in hippie clothing, both in prints and accessories. Flower crowns and garlands were worn as symbols of peace and harmony, inspired by the **flower power movement** that emerged as a form of anti-war protest. Floral embroidery adorned shirts, dresses, and bags, emphasizing the connection between the counterculture and nature.

Hippie style also blurred gender norms in fashion. Men adopted long hair, flowing shirts, and jewelry, while women embraced trousers, tunics, and unisex denim. This rejection of traditional gendered clothing reflected the counterculture's broader challenges to societal conventions around identity and roles. Clothing became a tool for expressing fluidity and individuality.

The **anti-establishment message** of hippie fashion extended to its use of vintage and secondhand clothing. Thrift stores and flea markets became popular sources for unique pieces, and mixing decades—Victorian lace blouses with 1940s trousers, for example—became a hallmark of the era's eclectic aesthetic. This approach to fashion was a direct critique of fast-changing, consumer-driven trends.

Natural beauty was central to the hippie look. Makeup, if worn, was minimal, with a focus on earthy tones and natural features. Women often skipped foundation and lipstick, favoring kohl eyeliner and a touch of lip balm. Hair was worn long and unstyled for both men and women, emphasizing a connection to nature and simplicity. Braids, often adorned with beads or flowers, became a popular way to enhance natural hairstyles.

Hippie fashion was not just about appearance; it was a **philosophical statement**. It rejected the artificiality of mainstream culture, embracing authenticity and sustainability. This ethos inspired later movements in ethical and sustainable fashion, demonstrating the long-term influence of the counterculture's values.

By the late 1970s, hippie style began evolving into more commercialized versions, influencing bohemian and disco trends. However, its core values—individuality, freedom, and a connection to nature—remained embedded in the culture of the decade.

Disco Glamour

Disco fashion emerged in the 1970s as a dazzling reflection of the nightclub scene, where individuality and expression collided with music and movement. Rooted in the vibrant nightlife of cities like New York and Los Angeles, disco style prioritized glamour, boldness, and the freedom to shine—literally and figuratively. The disco look embodied the hedonistic, carefree spirit of the era, with its emphasis on sensuality, self-expression, and a touch of excess.

The centerpiece of disco glamour was **shimmering fabrics and metallic finishes**. Satin, sequins, and lamé dominated the dance floor, reflecting the flashing lights of discotheques. Clothing was designed to catch the eye, with garments that glittered and glowed under the club's rotating disco balls. Gold, silver, and vibrant jewel tones like emerald green, cobalt blue, and fuchsia were staples of the disco palette, making bold color a defining feature of the style.

Women's disco fashion emphasized body-conscious designs. The **wrap dress**, made famous by **Diane von Fürstenberg**, was a wardrobe essential. Its figure-flattering silhouette, often made in bold prints or shimmering fabrics, transitioned effortlessly from day to night. Halter tops, plunging necklines, and backless dresses were equally popular, highlighting the body and encouraging movement. The focus on sensuality mirrored the freedom and confidence of the disco era.

For eveningwear, women often turned to **jumpsuits**, which became an iconic disco staple. These one-piece garments combined glamour and practicality, allowing for fluid motion on the dance floor. Jumpsuits featured dramatic elements like wide-legged pants, cinched waists, and high collars, often paired with metallic belts or bold accessories. Their versatility and impact made them a favorite among partygoers and celebrities alike.

Men's disco fashion was equally expressive. Suits, often in polyester or silk blends, came in vibrant colors and featured slim, tailored cuts with flared trousers. Shirts were typically unbuttoned to reveal the chest, accessorized with gold chains or medallions. The **leisure suit**, made popular by brands like Pierre Cardin, exemplified disco style for men. Its relaxed yet polished aesthetic was perfect for the nightlife scene, blending comfort with flair.

Platform shoes were a universal disco accessory, worn by both men and women. These elevated footwear choices added height, drama, and a sense of playfulness to any outfit. Women's platform heels often featured glitter or metallic finishes, while men's platforms, paired with flared trousers, added a theatrical edge to their look. The exaggerated proportions of platform shoes aligned with disco's love of the bold and unconventional.

Accessories in disco fashion were oversized and eye-catching. Hoop earrings, chunky bangles, and layered necklaces adorned dancers, enhancing the opulence of the era. Clutches and small handbags often featured metallic finishes or sequins to complement evening ensembles. Makeup was equally dramatic, with bold eyeshadow, thick eyeliner, and glossy lips adding to the polished yet flamboyant aesthetic.

Hairstyles completed the disco look, often emphasizing volume and texture. Women favored big, bouncy curls or sleek, straight styles that could hold their own on the dance floor. The **Afro**, worn proudly by both men and women, became a powerful symbol of cultural identity and self-expression within the disco scene, particularly among Black clubgoers. Men also embraced long hair, often styled with layers or a feathered look inspired by celebrities like John Travolta.

The influence of disco extended beyond the clubs and into mainstream fashion. Designers like Halston and Stephen Burrows drew inspiration from the disco scene, creating collections that celebrated the fluidity and freedom of the style. Halston, in particular, became synonymous with disco glamour, designing sleek, minimalist gowns and jumpsuits for clients like Bianca Jagger and Liza Minnelli. His use of luxurious fabrics like silk and chiffon elevated disco fashion, bringing it to the forefront of high society.

The connection between disco and celebrity culture was undeniable. The **Studio 54 nightclub in New York** became a fashion runway in its own right, with stars like Diana Ross, Cher, and Grace Jones showcasing extravagant looks. These iconic figures pushed the boundaries of disco fashion, embracing individuality and daring designs that inspired fans worldwide.

Disco's emphasis on **androgyny and inclusivity** also left a lasting impact on fashion. The unisex appeal of jumpsuits, platform shoes, and bold colors blurred traditional gender lines, reflecting the progressive attitudes of the disco scene. This fluidity in style celebrated individuality and self-expression, aligning with the era's broader social movements for equality and liberation.

At the end of the 1970s, disco fashion had evolved into a global phenomenon. Its glittering, unapologetic glamour defined an era where individuality and expression were celebrated on and off the dance floor. Even as the disco movement began to fade in the 1980s, its impact on fashion—its embrace of boldness, sensuality, and fun—remained a defining feature of the decade.

Punk Fashion

Punk fashion exploded in the mid-1970s as a radical statement of rebellion against mainstream culture. Emerging from the gritty streets of London and New York, it rejected the polished, glamorous aesthetics of disco and embraced a raw, DIY ethos. The punk style was as much about attitude as it was about clothing, reflecting the anger, disillusionment, and defiance of a generation dissatisfied with social norms and economic inequality.

The foundation of punk fashion was **deliberate nonconformity**. Ripped clothing, held together by safety pins, became a hallmark of the style. Jeans and T-shirts were slashed and torn, with the imperfections left visible as a rejection of polished, mass-produced fashion. Punks often customized their clothes with DIY embellishments like patches, studs, and provocative slogans, turning everyday garments into political and artistic statements.

Leather jackets became iconic within punk fashion. Decorated with spikes, chains, or painted logos, these jackets symbolized toughness and rebellion. Paired with skinny jeans, fishnet stockings, or tartan skirts, leather jackets offered a unifying element in a style defined by its chaos and individuality. Brands like **Schott** popularized the biker jacket, which quickly became synonymous with punk culture.

Tartan patterns were another staple of punk style, often used ironically to subvert their association with traditional British culture. Designers like **Vivienne Westwood** and Malcolm McLaren, who ran the boutique **SEX** in London, incorporated tartan into their collections, pairing it with leather and latex to create provocative, anarchic looks. Westwood's influence on punk fashion was transformative, blending high design with street-level rebellion.

Punk footwear was equally distinctive. **Doc Martens boots**, originally designed as workwear, were adopted by punks for their durability and utilitarian style. Combat boots and creepers also became popular, reflecting the movement's gritty, working-class roots. These shoes were often scuffed, painted, or adorned with metal accessories, adding to their rough, rebellious aesthetic.

Hair was a major form of self-expression in punk culture. Mohawks, spiked styles, and shaved heads defied mainstream beauty standards, while vibrant, unnatural hair colors like neon green or electric blue further emphasized individuality. Hair dye became a tool for creating bold, dramatic looks, often achieved with cheap, accessible products that aligned with punk's DIY philosophy.

Makeup in punk fashion was intentionally striking and unconventional. Heavy eyeliner, smudged mascara, and black lipstick challenged traditional notions of beauty. Gender norms were frequently subverted, with men wearing bold makeup and women adopting androgynous or aggressive styles. Punk makeup mirrored the movement's emphasis on defiance and personal expression.

Accessories completed the punk look. Safety pins, originally used as functional repairs, became jewelry, worn as earrings, necklaces, or brooches. Spiked collars and wristbands added a menacing edge, while chains and padlocks, often borrowed from hardware stores, became necklaces or belts. These industrial elements emphasized punk's raw, anti-establishment ethos.

Music was at the heart of punk culture, and fashion drew heavily from its energy. Bands like **The Sex Pistols**, **The Clash**, and **Ramones** not only shaped the sound of punk but also set its visual tone. Sid Vicious, Johnny Rotten, and Debbie Harry became style icons, influencing fans with their fearless, unpolished looks. Concerts and punk clubs served as informal runways, where fans showcased their creativity and pushed boundaries.

Punk fashion was deeply political, challenging societal norms and consumerism. Many punks deliberately rejected expensive clothing, instead favoring secondhand and thrifted items. Customization became a form of protest, with slogans, political patches, and provocative imagery turning outfits into walking manifestos. The movement's anarchic spirit extended to its rejection of traditional fashion hierarchies, emphasizing that anyone could participate in punk style.

At the end of the decade, punk fashion had begun influencing mainstream designers. Vivienne Westwood's work with the punk aesthetic brought it into high fashion, while labels like **Jean Paul Gaultier** incorporated punk-inspired elements into their collections. Despite its appropriation by the fashion industry, punk style retained its rebellious core, continuing to inspire subcultures and countercultural movements well into the following decades.

Ethnic Revival and Global Inspirations

The 1970s saw an **ethnic revival** in fashion, as designers and individuals embraced styles, patterns, and craftsmanship from around the globe. This movement reflected the decade's focus on individuality, self-expression, and a rejection of homogenized, mass-produced clothing. Drawing inspiration from diverse cultures, the ethnic revival introduced rich textures, bold prints, and traditional techniques into contemporary wardrobes, blending cultural appreciation with the free-spirited ethos of the era.

The rise of the ethnic revival was fueled by the counterculture movement's emphasis on authenticity and exploration. Many young people, dissatisfied with the conformity of Western consumer culture, sought alternative ways of living and dressing. This shift coincided with a broader interest in travel, cultural exchange, and Eastern philosophies. Fashion became a medium for expressing this global curiosity, with garments and accessories that celebrated craftsmanship and heritage.

Indian influences were particularly prominent in the ethnic revival. The popularity of Eastern spirituality, yoga, and meditation in the 1970s brought attention to India's rich textile traditions. **Kaftans** and tunics, often made from hand-printed cotton or silk, became wardrobe staples, prized for their comfort and elegance. Paisley patterns, originating from Persian and Indian designs, were widely used in everything from scarves to evening dresses, their intricate swirls symbolizing the exotic appeal of the East. **Sari-inspired gowns** appeared on runways and red carpets, blending traditional Indian silhouettes with Western glamour.

African aesthetics also were common in the ethnic revival. Designers incorporated **bold geometric patterns, vibrant colors, and intricate beadwork** into their collections. Dashikis, a traditional West African garment, became popular in both casual and formal settings, symbolizing pride in African heritage. Jewelry made from natural materials like wood, bone, and brass echoed the shapes and textures of African designs. These pieces were often oversized and sculptural, making them striking additions to minimalist or bohemian outfits.

The influence of **Native American culture** could be seen in fringe jackets, moccasins, and turquoise jewelry, which were widely adopted during this period. Beaded necklaces, inspired by indigenous craftsmanship, became common accessories, often worn layered over simple tops or dresses. Patterns inspired by Navajo weavings appeared in knitwear and outerwear, translating traditional motifs into wearable art. These designs were embraced not only for their visual appeal but also for their connection to the natural world, aligning with the environmental consciousness of the decade.

Middle Eastern and North African styles added another dimension to the ethnic revival. Kaftans and djellabas, with their flowing shapes and ornate embroidery, became symbols of effortless luxury. These garments, often made from lightweight fabrics like cotton or silk, were perfect for the relaxed, bohemian lifestyles that defined the 1970s. Designers like Yves Saint Laurent drew inspiration from Moroccan culture, incorporating elements like rich jewel tones, elaborate patterns, and gold-thread embellishments into their collections. His 1976 **"Ballet Russes"**

collection, although rooted in Russian folk costumes, showcased the broader trend of adapting traditional garments for high fashion.

The ethnic revival wasn't limited to clothing—it extended to **textiles and interior design**, reflecting a holistic embrace of global aesthetics. Ikat prints from Central Asia, Peruvian weavings, and Chinese silk patterns were used not only in garments but also in home decor, creating a seamless integration of global inspiration across lifestyle choices. Many of these textiles were handcrafted, emphasizing the movement's appreciation for artistry and tradition.

Handcrafted elements were central to the ethnic revival. The rise of **DIY culture** during the 1970s encouraged people to experiment with traditional techniques like weaving, embroidery, and batik. This hands-on approach to fashion allowed individuals to create unique pieces, blending cultural motifs with personal expression. Patchwork garments, for example, often combined fabrics from different parts of the world, creating a collage of patterns and colors that celebrated diversity.

The ethnic revival also aligned with the growing **feminist movement**, which encouraged women to embrace clothing that prioritized comfort and freedom over restrictive, Westernized ideals of femininity. Flowing dresses, loose trousers, and unstructured silhouettes borrowed from non-Western styles allowed for greater ease of movement and self-expression. These garments rejected the rigid tailoring and constricting designs of previous decades, reflecting a broader shift toward liberation in fashion and society.

Japanese influences became particularly prominent in the later 1970s. Designers like **Issey Miyake** and **Kenzo Takada** brought traditional Japanese techniques and aesthetics to the international stage, blending East and West in innovative ways. Miyake's work, for example, emphasized pleating and minimalist design, inspired by both ancient Japanese craftsmanship and modern technology. Kimono-inspired jackets and wide obi belts appeared in high fashion and streetwear, reinterpreted to suit contemporary tastes.

The ethnic revival also highlighted the influence of **South American cultures** on 1970s fashion. Ponchos and capes, inspired by traditional Andean garments, became popular outerwear options, offering warmth and versatility. These pieces often featured handwoven fabrics with geometric patterns or stripes, showcasing the craftsmanship of indigenous communities. Alpaca wool, prized for its softness and durability, became a sought-after material for sweaters, scarves, and blankets.

As interest in global fashion grew, travel became a major driver of style. Many individuals collected garments, textiles, and jewelry during trips abroad, incorporating these pieces into their wardrobes as symbols of cultural exchange. The popularity of ethnic-inspired fashion also led to the rise of boutique shops and marketplaces that specialized in importing handmade items from around the world. These spaces provided a direct connection to artisans and their traditions, reinforcing the authenticity of the movement.

The ethnic revival was not without its complexities. While it celebrated cultural diversity and craftsmanship, it also raised questions about appropriation and commercialization. Many traditional designs were adapted or mass-produced for Western audiences, often divorced from their original cultural contexts. This tension highlighted the fine line between appreciation and exploitation, a debate that continues in fashion today.

Despite these challenges, the ethnic revival of the 1970s left a lasting legacy. It expanded the boundaries of fashion, introducing a global perspective that celebrated individuality and craftsmanship. By embracing the richness of cultural traditions, the movement challenged the dominance of Western fashion, creating a more inclusive and expressive landscape.

CHAPTER 13: THE POWER DRESSING OF THE 1980S

Shoulder Pads and Corporate Looks

The 1980s was a decade defined by ambition and assertiveness, and fashion reflected the competitive environment of the corporate world. **Power dressing** became the dominant style for professionals, particularly women entering male-dominated spaces. At the heart of this look were **shoulder pads**, which transformed the silhouette and symbolized strength, authority, and confidence. The combination of structured tailoring, bold proportions, and a polished aesthetic created a uniform for success.

Shoulder pads were the defining feature of 1980s power dressing. These foam or fabric inserts were sewn into jackets, blazers, and dresses to create a strong, angular shoulder line. The wide shoulders contrasted with a nipped-in waist, creating a V-shaped silhouette that conveyed authority and competence. The exaggerated shoulders drew inspiration from military uniforms and 1940s fashion, but the 1980s took this feature to new extremes, making it an essential part of corporate attire.

For women, shoulder pads represented more than just a fashion trend—they were a statement of empowerment. As more women entered the workforce and climbed the corporate ladder, they adopted a style that visually aligned them with male colleagues while maintaining a sense of femininity. The broadened shoulders suggested strength, while the fitted waists and tailored skirts balanced the look with a touch of elegance. Designers like Giorgio Armani led this movement, creating sleek, minimalist suits that became staples of the power wardrobe.

The **power suit** was the cornerstone of corporate looks in the 1980s. Women's suits often featured sharp lapels, double-breasted jackets, and pencil skirts that ended just above the knee. Trousers became more common as well, marking a shift in women's fashion toward practicality and equality. Fabrics like wool and gabardine gave these suits structure, while neutral colors like black, navy, and gray dominated the palette, signaling professionalism and seriousness.

Men's corporate fashion in the 1980s also emphasized sharp tailoring and clean lines. **Double-breasted suits** with broad shoulders and wide lapels were a popular choice, reflecting the same desire for authority and dominance seen in women's power dressing. Pinstripes became a hallmark of Wall Street style, reinforcing the image of success and ambition. Accessories like suspenders, pocket squares, and bold ties added personality without straying from the polished aesthetic.

The emphasis on structured silhouettes extended to **blouses and dresses**, which often featured shoulder pads to maintain the angular lines of the era. Women paired tailored blazers with **pussy-bow blouses**, which added a touch of femininity while still adhering to the corporate uniform. These blouses, often made of silk or polyester, came in bold colors or prints, offering a bit of individuality within the structured confines of professional attire.

Accessories were carefully chosen to complement the power dressing aesthetic. Women wore **simple, geometric jewelry**, such as gold hoop earrings or chunky bracelets, that mirrored the sharp lines of their suits. Belts with bold buckles cinched the waist, emphasizing the hourglass figure within the strong-shouldered silhouette. Handbags were structured and practical, with designers like Hermès and Gucci offering styles that balanced elegance with utility.

Hair and makeup completed the corporate look, reinforcing the polished and confident image. Hairstyles were voluminous, with blowouts and perms creating height and drama. The emphasis on big hair echoed the broader proportions of the clothing. Makeup focused on bold eyes and defined cheeks, with red or mauve lipstick adding a pop of color. These choices projected a sense of control and poise, essential qualities for navigating the competitive environments of the 1980s workplace.

Television shows like *Dynasty* and *Dallas* popularized the power dressing trend, showcasing characters dressed in exaggerated silhouettes and luxurious fabrics. Joan Collins' portrayal of Alexis Carrington in *Dynasty* epitomized the 1980s corporate look, with her wardrobe of sharply tailored suits, oversized jewelry, and dramatic makeup. These shows amplified the allure of power dressing, making it aspirational for audiences around the world.

Designers were important in shaping the aesthetic of power dressing. **Giorgio Armani** became synonymous with the 1980s corporate wardrobe, offering understated yet impeccably tailored suits that appealed to both men and women. His use of neutral tones and luxurious fabrics created a timeless elegance that transcended seasonal trends. **Donna Karan** also emerged as a key figure, designing versatile pieces that catered to professional women. Her **Seven Easy Pieces** collection in 1985 revolutionized workwear by offering a mix-and-match wardrobe that combined comfort and sophistication.

While power dressing dominated the corporate world, it also faced criticism for its uniformity and the pressure it placed on women to conform to a male-centric standard of professionalism. Some argued that the emphasis on broad shoulders and tailored suits forced women to adopt a more masculine appearance to succeed in the workplace. However, others viewed it as a necessary step toward equality, providing women with the visual tools to command respect and authority.

The influence of power dressing extended beyond the office. Evening wear in the 1980s borrowed elements from corporate fashion, incorporating structured shoulders and angular lines into gowns and cocktail dresses. Sequins, metallic fabrics, and dramatic silhouettes added glamour to the strong, confident look of the decade. This crossover between day and evening wear highlighted the cultural dominance of the power dressing aesthetic.

As the 1980s progressed, the proportions of power dressing became increasingly exaggerated. Shoulder pads grew larger, lapels widened, and colors brightened, reflecting the era's embrace of excess and boldness. By the end of the decade, these extreme styles began to wane, but their impact on fashion was undeniable. The emphasis on structure, tailoring, and professional polish reshaped the way people dressed for work and beyond, leaving a legacy that continues to influence modern fashion.

The Influence of Supermodels

The 1980s marked the rise of the **supermodel**, a new phenomenon that transformed the fashion industry and influenced how power dressing evolved throughout the decade. These women were more than just faces on runways—they were global icons who embodied the bold, aspirational spirit of the 1980s. Their presence in advertisements, editorials, and public life shaped how people perceived and adopted trends, particularly the polished, confident look associated with power dressing.

Supermodels like **Cindy Crawford**, **Naomi Campbell**, **Christy Turlington**, and **Linda Evangelista** became household names during this era. Unlike earlier models, whose influence was confined to fashion magazines and shows, these women became celebrities in their own right. Their ability to command attention in a room mirrored the assertiveness of 1980s fashion. Designers and brands capitalized on their star power, using them to sell the image of strength, glamour, and success that defined the decade.

The rise of supermodels coincided with the growing dominance of luxury brands in shaping trends. High-profile campaigns featuring supermodels wearing power suits, structured evening gowns, and bold accessories reinforced the aesthetics of power dressing. Designers like Giorgio Armani, Thierry Mugler, and Claude Montana embraced the supermodel phenomenon, creating collections that amplified their commanding presence. Armani's understated tailoring, for instance, looked even more striking when worn by models who exuded confidence and poise.

Runway shows in the 1980s became theatrical productions, with supermodels as the main attraction. Designers used these shows to emphasize the drama and precision of their creations, with structured shoulders, cinched waists, and dramatic fabrics taking center stage. The models' ability to convey authority through their walk and posture amplified the message of power dressing. The catwalks became arenas where confidence and glamour were celebrated, making the clothing more aspirational for the audience.

Editorials in leading fashion magazines like *Vogue*, *Elle*, and *Harper's Bazaar* were influential in popularizing the supermodel aesthetic. Photographers like **Steven Meisel** and **Herb Ritts** captured these models in powerfully posed images, often featuring them in tailored blazers, bold jewel tones, and striking accessories. These images conveyed a narrative of empowerment and sophistication, inspiring readers to adopt elements of power dressing in their own wardrobes.

Advertising campaigns elevated the connection between supermodels and consumer aspirations. Brands like Chanel, Versace, and Ralph Lauren leaned into the polished, professional aesthetic of power dressing, presenting it as the ultimate expression of success and modernity. Supermodels appeared in these ads not just as mannequins for the clothing but as embodiments of the lifestyle the brand was selling. Their presence suggested that wearing these clothes would grant the wearer the same confidence and allure.

Fitness and body image were also central to the supermodel phenomenon of the 1980s. The rise of aerobics and the emphasis on health aligned with the decade's focus on ambition and self-improvement. Supermodels epitomized this ideal, with toned, athletic physiques that complemented the structured, body-conscious designs of power dressing. Their influence encouraged women to embrace a more active lifestyle, which in turn shaped fashion trends like structured sportswear and body-con dresses.

The influence of supermodels wasn't confined to high fashion; it trickled down into everyday style. Women across the globe looked to these icons for inspiration, emulating their hairstyles, makeup, and wardrobe choices. Big hair, bold makeup, and tailored blazers became staples of power dressing, reflecting the supermodels' polished yet assertive look. The accessibility of these trends reinforced the idea that anyone could channel the confidence and glamour associated with the era.

Television and film further amplified the impact of supermodels. Appearances in music videos, talk shows, and movies brought them into mainstream culture, making their style more relatable and desirable. Naomi Campbell's runway strut, Cindy Crawford's all-American appeal, and Linda Evangelista's high-fashion versatility became defining elements of 1980s fashion, influencing not just what people wore but how they carried themselves.

Sportswear and Street Style

While power dressing dominated the corporate world, **sportswear and street style** emerged as equally influential trends in 1980s fashion, reflecting the era's focus on individuality and self-expression. These styles offered a more casual counterpoint to the polished suits and shoulder pads of the workplace, drawing inspiration from fitness culture, hip-hop, and urban streetwear.

The fitness boom of the 1980s revolutionized sportswear. The rise of aerobics, spearheaded by figures like Jane Fonda, introduced colorful, body-hugging athletic gear into mainstream fashion. **Leggings, leotards, and sweatbands** became staples not just for exercise but also for casual outings. Bright colors, neon accents, and bold patterns defined this look, which prioritized movement and energy. The stretchy, form-fitting fabrics of sportswear complemented the body-conscious aesthetic of the decade.

Tracksuits, once relegated to gym wear, became fashionable thanks to brands like Adidas and Puma. These pieces, often made from shiny materials like nylon, featured bold stripes and logos that added visual impact. Paired with sneakers, tracksuits blurred the lines between functional athletic wear and everyday style, making them a staple of street fashion.

The rise of hip-hop culture in the 1980s further propelled sportswear into the spotlight. Artists like **Run-D.M.C.** and **LL Cool J** turned items like shell-toe Adidas sneakers, Kangol hats, and oversized jackets into symbols of urban style. The hip-hop aesthetic celebrated individuality and creativity, encouraging fans to personalize their looks with gold chains, graffiti-inspired prints, and bold accessories. This movement made sportswear not just a fashion choice but a statement of cultural identity.

Sneakers became a defining element of street style in the 1980s. The release of the **Air Jordan** by Nike in 1984 transformed sneakers into coveted fashion items. Athletes like Michael Jordan and celebrities alike wore these shoes, making them a symbol of status and style. Brands like Reebok, Converse, and Fila also capitalized on the trend, creating sneakers that combined performance with bold designs. Sneaker culture emerged as a key facet of streetwear, laying the foundation for its evolution in the following decades.

Denim also was common in 1980s street style. **Baggy jeans, acid-washed finishes, and high-waisted cuts** became popular, reflecting the decade's love of experimentation. Brands like Levi's and Guess offered denim pieces that appealed to both men and women, often styled with graphic T-shirts or oversized sweaters. This casual, mix-and-match approach to fashion celebrated individuality, allowing wearers to create unique looks that reflected their personalities.

Accessories in street style were bold and often oversized. **Chunky gold jewelry**, inspired by hip-hop culture, became a signature element of urban fashion. Large hoop earrings, layered necklaces, and statement belts added flair to even the simplest outfits. Backpacks and fanny packs, often worn in bright colors or flashy materials, combined practicality with style, aligning with the active, on-the-go lifestyle of the 1980s.

The influence of street style extended to hair and makeup. Hairstyles like the **Jheri curl**, high-top fade, and side ponytail reflected the playful and experimental nature of the era. Makeup often featured bold eyeshadow, glossy lips, and dramatic blush, mirroring the vibrant colors of sportswear and accessories. These choices emphasized self-expression, encouraging people to take risks and embrace their individuality.

Television shows like *Miami Vice*, *Fresh Prince of Bel-Air*, and music videos by artists like Run-D.M.C. and Madonna captured the bold creativity and dynamic energy of 1980s street style, propelling it into the mainstream. *Miami Vice* popularized casual yet sleek urban looks, with pastel suits and T-shirts inspiring a blend of streetwear and upscale fashion. Meanwhile, Madonna's rebellious style in videos like "Borderline" and "Lucky Star" embraced layered jewelry, mesh tops, and oversized silhouettes, reflecting the decade's experimental spirit.

This growing visibility helped bridge the gap between high fashion and urban culture. Designers like Jean-Paul Gaultier and Vivienne Westwood began incorporating street-inspired elements into their collections, giving streetwear a platform on global runways.

CHAPTER 14: THE MINIMALISM OF THE 1990S

Grunge Fashion

Grunge fashion emerged in the early 1990s as a visual extension of the alternative music scene centered in Seattle. It rejected the polished, opulent looks of the 1980s, embracing instead a stripped-down, anti-consumerist aesthetic. Rooted in practicality and rebellion, grunge fashion was a mix of thrift-store finds, unkempt layering, and androgynous silhouettes that challenged the traditional ideas of glamour and style.

The **hallmark of grunge fashion** was its deliberate nonchalance. Flannel shirts, oversized sweaters, and ripped jeans dominated wardrobes, offering a casual, almost careless look. These pieces were often sourced from secondhand shops, reflecting both the DIY ethos of the grunge movement and its rejection of fast fashion. Comfort took precedence over trends, with garments chosen for their utility rather than their statement.

Plaid flannel shirts became synonymous with grunge, thanks to their association with the Pacific Northwest's working-class roots. Originally worn for practicality in cold, damp climates, these shirts were co-opted by musicians like Kurt Cobain of Nirvana and Eddie Vedder of Pearl Jam, becoming iconic symbols of the genre. Often worn oversized or layered over band T-shirts, flannels embodied the unpretentious attitude of the movement.

Denim was another cornerstone of grunge fashion. **Ripped, faded, or baggy jeans** were preferred, emphasizing wear and authenticity over pristine finishes. Jeans were often paired with worn-out sneakers or combat boots, such as Doc Martens, adding a utilitarian edge. The emphasis on distressed or vintage clothing reflected the movement's focus on individuality and its disdain for the excess of the previous decade.

Layering was central to the grunge look. People combined mismatched textures and patterns, layering loose-fitting garments like thermal shirts, oversized cardigans, and long skirts. The goal wasn't cohesion—it was a sense of disarray that mirrored the raw, emotional themes of grunge music. Clothing was often gender-neutral, with both men and women adopting similar silhouettes, blurring the lines between traditional masculinity and femininity.

Footwear choices in grunge fashion reflected the same practical, anti-fashion ethos. **Doc Martens** became iconic for their durability and connection to punk and counterculture movements. Worn scuffed and well-used, they reinforced the grunge aesthetic of rejecting polished appearances. Sneakers, particularly Converse All-Stars, were another staple, chosen for their simplicity and affordability.

Accessories in grunge fashion were minimal but meaningful. Beanies, often slouchy or oversized, were a popular choice, adding warmth and a casual vibe. Chain necklaces, chokers, and simple leather bands occasionally appeared, but the overall look avoided overt decoration. Backpacks, often weathered and utilitarian, replaced handbags, aligning with the movement's practical mindset.

The influence of grunge extended to hair and makeup. Hair was typically natural, unstyled, and often intentionally messy. Long, unkempt locks for both men and women became a hallmark of the look, while dyed hair in unconventional colors like green, blue, or pink added an element of rebellion. Makeup was minimal or deliberately smudged, with dark eyeliner and neutral lips reflecting a raw, unaffected appearance.

Grunge fashion also emphasized **secondhand and vintage clothing**, reinforcing its anti-consumerist stance. Thrift stores became the go-to destination for grunge enthusiasts, who valued the individuality and sustainability of reused clothing. This approach stood in stark contrast to the designer-driven trends of the 1980s, marking a cultural shift toward rejecting mainstream consumerism.

While grunge was deeply rooted in music and youth culture, it didn't take long for the fashion industry to capitalize on the trend. Designers like Marc Jacobs famously incorporated grunge elements into high fashion, with his 1992 collection for Perry Ellis showcasing flannel shirts, knitted beanies, and floral slip dresses layered over T-shirts. This move drew criticism from grunge purists, who saw the commercial appropriation of their style as contradictory to its anti-establishment roots.

Women's grunge fashion often included **slip dresses**, paired with combat boots or sneakers for an intentionally mismatched look. These lightweight, delicate garments contrasted sharply with the rugged flannels and knits, creating an aesthetic that was both gritty and soft. Tights with intentional runs or tears added to the undone quality, while oversized jackets or cardigans balanced the femininity of the dresses.

Grunge's influence wasn't confined to the Pacific Northwest. The movement spread globally, aided by the success of bands like Nirvana, Soundgarden, and Alice in Chains. Their music videos and live performances served as visual guides to the grunge aesthetic, inspiring fans to adopt the same clothing and attitude. By the mid-1990s, grunge had become a dominant force in mainstream culture, reshaping how people thought about fashion and individuality.

Despite its anti-fashion origins, grunge fashion eventually infiltrated advertising and pop culture, appearing in magazines and television shows. Retailers like The Gap and Urban Outfitters began offering pre-distressed jeans and flannel-inspired pieces, making grunge accessible to a wider audience. This commercialization diluted some of the movement's authenticity, but it also solidified its impact on fashion history.

Grunge fashion reflected the broader cultural themes of the 1990s. It was a reaction to the consumerism and excess of the 1980s, offering an alternative that embraced authenticity, imperfection, and emotional expression. It celebrated individuality over conformity, making it a defining movement for a generation questioning traditional values and norms.

The Influence of Designers Like Calvin Klein

Calvin Klein was a central figure in the **minimalist movement of the 1990s**, shaping a new aesthetic that emphasized simplicity, clean lines, and understated elegance. His approach rejected the excess and boldness of the 1980s, offering instead a pared-down style that resonated with the era's shift toward subtlety and refinement. His work not only defined 1990s fashion but also set a standard for modern minimalism.

Klein's designs were characterized by their **neutral color palettes** and simple silhouettes. He used shades like white, black, gray, and beige to create a clean, timeless look. His collections avoided embellishments or ornate details, focusing instead on impeccable tailoring and high-quality fabrics. This approach was revolutionary in an industry often dominated by dramatic, over-the-top designs, making minimalism a statement of sophistication.

One of Calvin Klein's most iconic contributions was his **underwear line**, which became synonymous with 1990s minimalism. Introduced in the late 1980s but gaining widespread popularity in the 1990s, his simple cotton briefs and boxer briefs featured clean lines and the brand's name prominently displayed on the waistband. The campaign for this line, featuring images of a young Mark Wahlberg and Kate Moss, captured the decade's aesthetic perfectly: sleek, androgynous, and unadorned. The minimalist design and provocative marketing elevated underwear from a functional garment to a fashion statement.

Klein's ad campaigns were prominent in defining his influence. The black-and-white imagery, often featuring bare, natural-looking models like Kate Moss, aligned with his minimalist ethos. These campaigns stripped fashion photography of excess, focusing instead on the beauty of simplicity and the body. Klein's marketing aesthetic wasn't just about clothing—it was about a lifestyle, one that emphasized effortless cool and authenticity.

His **ready-to-wear collections** for men and women also epitomized 1990s minimalism. Slim-cut suits, slip dresses, and simple knitwear dominated his runway shows, presenting a vision of modernity that was both accessible and aspirational. The slip dress, in particular, became a defining garment of the decade, popularized by Klein and worn by celebrities like Gwyneth Paltrow and Carolyn Bessette-Kennedy. Made of silk or satin, these dresses hugged the body with a delicate yet unfussy allure, embodying the decade's focus on quiet luxury.

Klein's designs reflected broader cultural shifts, particularly in how people thought about gender and sexuality. His clothes often blurred traditional distinctions, with androgynous cuts and styles that appealed to both men and women. This approach mirrored the growing conversations around gender fluidity in the 1990s and positioned Calvin Klein as a brand that was ahead of its time.

His influence extended beyond fashion to **fragrance**, with iconic scents like CK One redefining the industry. Launched in 1994, CK One was a unisex fragrance marketed as gender-neutral, further emphasizing Klein's commitment to inclusivity and minimalism. The minimalist packaging, with its frosted glass bottle and clean typography, reinforced the brand's aesthetic while appealing to a new generation of consumers seeking authenticity.

Calvin Klein's impact on fashion also came from his ability to **merge high fashion with commercial success**. While his collections were celebrated on runways, his diffusion lines, such as CK and Calvin Klein Jeans, made his minimalist style accessible to a wider audience. These lines offered affordable, well-designed pieces that adhered to the same principles of simplicity and quality, ensuring that Klein's vision reached beyond luxury markets.

While Calvin Klein's name became almost synonymous with minimalism, his influence wasn't isolated. Designers like Jil Sander and Helmut Lang shared similar philosophies, but Klein's branding and marketing genius made him the most recognizable face of the movement. His ability to distill complex design into universally appealing pieces solidified his place as a defining designer of the decade.

Globalization of Fashion Brands

The **1990s marked the globalization of fashion brands**, as advances in technology, communication, and transportation allowed designers to expand their reach across continents. This decade saw the rise of international flagship stores, collaborations with celebrities, and marketing strategies tailored for a global audience. The minimalist aesthetic of the 1990s, with its universal appeal, made it easier for brands to resonate with consumers worldwide.

Globalization allowed brands to create **cohesive identities** that transcended regional differences. Companies like Calvin Klein, Prada, and Giorgio Armani capitalized on the decade's minimalist trends, presenting sleek, modern designs that appealed to a broad spectrum of cultures. Neutral palettes, simple silhouettes, and timeless styles became the language of global fashion, bridging gaps between diverse markets.

Luxury brands invested heavily in **flagship stores** in major cities around the world. Gucci, for example, opened lavish boutiques in Tokyo, New York, and Paris, creating spaces that reflected the brand's ethos while appealing to local tastes. These stores weren't just places to shop—they were experiences, designed to immerse consumers in the world of the brand. The minimalist interiors, often featuring clean lines and high-quality materials, mirrored the designs on display, creating a seamless narrative.

Advertising campaigns became global phenomena, as brands began investing in large-scale productions that could be adapted for multiple markets. Calvin Klein's campaigns, featuring stark black-and-white imagery and universal themes of youth and rebellion, resonated across cultures. Similarly, Prada and Armani used their campaigns to project a sense of timeless sophistication, ensuring that their branding remained consistent no matter the location.

The rise of **supermodels** further fueled the globalization of fashion brands. Figures like Naomi Campbell, Cindy Crawford, and Claudia Schiffer became recognizable around the world, bringing international appeal to the brands they represented. These models traveled across continents for runway shows, ad campaigns, and public appearances, ensuring that their influence—and the brands they endorsed—reached every corner of the globe.

Advancements in communication technology, particularly the internet, made it easier for brands to connect with consumers worldwide. While e-commerce was still in its infancy, the ability to showcase collections online marked the beginning of a new era for global fashion. Designers could now reach audiences who had never set foot in Paris, Milan, or New York, democratizing access to high fashion.

Globalization also encouraged **collaborations and partnerships**, as brands sought to tailor their offerings to different markets. For example, Japanese fashion became increasingly influential during the 1990s, with designers like Yohji Yamamoto and Issey Miyake gaining international acclaim. Western brands took note, incorporating Japanese-inspired minimalism into their collections and creating cross-cultural collaborations that enriched the industry.

The expansion of fast fashion giants like Zara and H&M was another key aspect of globalization in the 1990s. These companies mastered the art of producing runway-inspired clothing quickly and affordably, making trends accessible to consumers around the world. Their minimalist designs, often influenced by high-fashion brands, resonated with the era's aesthetic while appealing to a mass market.

The global reach of fashion also reshaped **production and supply chains**. Many luxury brands began outsourcing manufacturing to countries with lower labor costs, such as China and India. While this allowed for greater efficiency and scalability, it also raised questions about ethics and sustainability, concerns that would gain prominence in the following decades.

Celebrities became influential for globalizing fashion brands. In the 1990s, stars like Madonna, Kate Moss, and Gwyneth Paltrow were closely associated with specific designers, wearing their pieces on red carpets and in magazines. These endorsements helped brands like Versace and Calvin Klein reach international audiences, as fans sought to emulate their favorite celebrities' style.

The globalization of fashion also led to a growing appreciation for **regional aesthetics**. While Western brands dominated the market, the 1990s saw increasing interest in designs from Asia, Africa, and the Middle East. Traditional techniques and patterns from these regions began influencing collections, adding depth and diversity to the global fashion landscape.

Toward the end of the 1990s, the globalization of fashion brands had transformed the industry. The minimalist aesthetic, with its universal appeal, became the bridge between cultures, allowing designers to reach new markets while maintaining their core identities. This global interconnectedness laid the foundation for the digital and fast-paced fashion world of the 21st century.

CHAPTER 15: 21ST-CENTURY FASHION TRENDS

Sustainability and Ethical Fashion

Sustainability and ethical fashion have become defining movements of 21st-century fashion, reshaping how clothing is designed, produced, and consumed. As concerns about climate change, environmental degradation, and labor rights grew, the fashion industry faced increasing scrutiny for its role in these issues. Consumers, activists, and innovators began pushing for a new standard—one that valued the planet and people as much as profits.

One of the main drivers of sustainability in fashion is the **environmental impact of fast fashion**. The rise of fast fashion in the early 2000s led to an unprecedented acceleration of production cycles, with brands introducing dozens of collections per year. This model relies on cheap, synthetic fabrics like polyester, which shed microplastics into waterways and are derived from fossil fuels. Additionally, the high volume of clothing produced often leads to waste, with millions of tons of textiles ending up in landfills annually.

Sustainable fashion addresses these problems by focusing on **eco-friendly materials and processes**. Designers are turning to organic cotton, hemp, and bamboo as alternatives to conventional fabrics. Recycled materials are also gaining popularity. Brands like Patagonia and Adidas have pioneered the use of recycled polyester made from plastic bottles, turning waste into wearable garments. Similarly, some companies use deadstock fabric—unused textiles from previous production runs—to reduce waste.

The concept of **circular fashion** is central to sustainability. It promotes keeping garments in use for as long as possible through recycling, upcycling, and resale. Brands like Eileen Fisher and Stella McCartney embrace circular fashion by designing high-quality, timeless pieces that can be repaired or remade into new products. Online resale platforms like ThredUp and Vestiaire Collective have further popularized the idea, allowing consumers to buy and sell pre-owned clothing easily.

Another significant shift is the rise of **slow fashion**, which prioritizes quality over quantity. This movement encourages consumers to invest in fewer, better-made items that last longer, reducing the need for constant replacement. Many slow fashion brands focus on craftsmanship and ethical production, creating garments that are both durable and timeless. By reducing overproduction, slow fashion directly counters the wastefulness of fast fashion.

Labor ethics are equally important in the sustainability movement. High-profile tragedies, such as the 2013 collapse of the **Rana Plaza garment factory in**

Bangladesh, exposed the unsafe conditions and low wages endured by many workers in the global supply chain. In response, brands began committing to greater transparency. Labels like People Tree and Everlane publish detailed information about their factories and worker policies, ensuring consumers can make informed choices.

Technology has also enabled progress in sustainable fashion. Innovations like **3D knitting** allow garments to be made with zero waste, using only the exact amount of material needed. Similarly, biofabrication has introduced materials like lab-grown leather and spider silk, offering sustainable alternatives to animal products and synthetics. These breakthroughs not only reduce resource consumption but also open new possibilities for design.

Water conservation is another critical focus. Traditional textile production is notoriously water-intensive, with processes like cotton farming and dyeing consuming vast amounts of water. To address this, brands are adopting techniques like waterless dyeing and closed-loop systems that recycle water within production facilities. Levi's, for example, has developed a denim manufacturing process that uses significantly less water while still delivering the same quality.

Consumer behavior has been a driving force behind these changes. Millennials and Gen Z, in particular, have shown a strong preference for brands that align with their values. Social media has amplified this trend, with platforms like Instagram and TikTok raising awareness about sustainable practices and exposing unethical ones. Hashtags like #WhoMadeMyClothes, popularized by the **Fashion Revolution** movement, encourage consumers to question the origins of their garments and demand accountability.

Local production has also gained traction as a sustainable option. By manufacturing garments closer to their markets, brands can reduce the environmental impact of shipping and foster stronger relationships with their workers. This approach also supports regional economies and preserves traditional craftsmanship. Labels like Reformation and Christy Dawn highlight their local production processes, emphasizing the value of community and sustainability.

Efforts to tackle **textile waste** have led to innovative recycling programs. Some brands, such as H&M and Zara, have introduced take-back schemes where customers can return old clothing to be recycled into new fibers or repurposed into other products. While these initiatives are a step forward, critics argue they must be paired with reduced production to have a meaningful impact.

Collaboration between governments, non-profits, and the fashion industry has helped advance sustainability. The **United Nations' Fashion Industry Charter for Climate Action**, launched in 2018, aims to achieve net-zero emissions in the industry by 2050. Similarly, organizations like the Ellen MacArthur Foundation promote circular economy principles, encouraging brands to adopt more sustainable practices across their supply chains.

Education has become key in driving ethical fashion forward. Initiatives like Fashion Revolution Week and sustainable design programs in fashion schools teach consumers and aspiring designers about the importance of responsible practices. These efforts help embed sustainability into the DNA of future generations, ensuring the movement continues to grow.

Sustainability and ethical fashion have reshaped the industry, forcing brands to reconsider their impact on the world. This shift has not only changed how clothing is made but also how it is valued, moving away from disposability toward lasting quality and purpose.

The Rise of Fast Fashion

The 21st century witnessed the meteoric rise of **fast fashion**, a model built on rapid production cycles, low-cost materials, and a relentless push to meet ever-changing consumer demands. Fast fashion revolutionized the industry, democratizing access to trendy clothing but also introducing significant environmental and ethical challenges.

Fast fashion brands like Zara, H&M, and Forever 21 perfected a system that shortened the time from design to retail. Traditional fashion cycles, which once revolved around two main seasons, spring/summer and fall/winter, were replaced by **micro-seasons**, with new collections arriving every few weeks. This speed-to-market strategy enabled brands to respond to trends almost instantly, allowing consumers to replicate runway or celebrity looks at a fraction of the cost.

Central to fast fashion's success was its reliance on **globalized production networks**. By outsourcing manufacturing to countries with low labor costs, brands minimized expenses while maximizing output. Factories in countries like Bangladesh, Vietnam, and China became hubs for fast fashion production, enabling companies to churn out massive quantities of clothing at unprecedented speeds. However, this reliance on cheap labor often led to unsafe working conditions and exploitation, sparking global debates about the ethics of fast fashion.

The affordability of fast fashion made high-style accessible to the masses. Instead of saving up for a single designer piece, consumers could purchase multiple items for the same price. This shift fundamentally altered shopping habits, fostering a culture of **disposability**, where clothing was often worn only a few times before being discarded. As a result, the volume of textile waste skyrocketed, with landfills overwhelmed by cheaply made garments.

Fast fashion's **supply chain innovations** were another key driver of its dominance. Brands implemented just-in-time manufacturing, producing smaller batches of items and restocking only the bestsellers. This approach reduced excess inventory while encouraging impulse purchases, as consumers feared missing out on limited stock. Data analytics became critical, with companies using real-time sales data to adjust production and predict future trends.

Social media amplified the demand for fast fashion. Platforms like Instagram and Pinterest showcased constantly evolving styles, fueling the desire for new outfits. The rise of influencers, who often posted daily outfits featuring affordable brands, reinforced the appeal of inexpensive, trendy clothing. Fast fashion brands capitalized on this by collaborating with influencers and running targeted ads, further embedding themselves into the digital landscape.

While fast fashion provided accessibility, it came at a cost to the environment. The reliance on synthetic fabrics like polyester, which are derived from fossil fuels, contributed to greenhouse gas emissions and microplastic pollution. Additionally, the water-intensive processes used for dyeing and finishing fabrics strained natural resources. Brands faced mounting pressure from activists and consumers to address these issues, leading some to launch **sustainability initiatives**, such as clothing recycling programs or the use of eco-friendly materials. However, critics argued these efforts were often token gestures rather than meaningful changes.

The COVID-19 pandemic disrupted fast fashion's momentum, exposing vulnerabilities in its supply chains and shifting consumer priorities toward sustainability and quality. Many consumers began reevaluating their shopping habits, turning to secondhand platforms and local brands. Despite this, fast fashion remained a dominant force, adapting to new realities by investing in e-commerce and digital marketing.

Fast fashion transformed how people interacted with clothing, making trends more accessible but raising critical questions about ethics, sustainability, and the true cost of affordable style. Its impact reshaped not only the industry but also global culture, leaving a complex legacy that continues to evolve.

Digital and Influencer Impact on Style

The **digital revolution** and the rise of influencers have profoundly shaped 21st-century fashion, altering how trends are created, consumed, and shared. Social media platforms, blogs, and e-commerce transformed fashion from an industry once controlled by designers and magazines into a participatory space where anyone with a smartphone could influence style.

The emergence of **Instagram in 2010** marked a turning point in how fashion was presented. Unlike traditional media, which offered polished, curated editorials, Instagram allowed for immediate, user-generated content. This democratized fashion, giving independent designers, small brands, and everyday users a platform to showcase their style. Hashtags like #OOTD (Outfit of the Day) encouraged users to share their looks, fostering a sense of community and sparking new trends.

Influencers became the central figures in this new ecosystem. Unlike traditional celebrities, influencers cultivated direct relationships with their followers, building trust and relatability. Their ability to showcase outfits in real-life settings made fashion more accessible, breaking down the exclusivity of runway looks. Micro-influencers, with smaller but highly engaged audiences, often had outsized impacts, particularly in niche markets like sustainable fashion or streetwear.

Digital platforms blurred the lines between advertising and personal content. Brands began partnering with influencers to reach their target demographics, offering free products or paid sponsorships in exchange for promotion. These collaborations proved highly effective, as followers perceived influencer endorsements as more authentic than traditional ads. Fashion Nova, for example, grew rapidly by leveraging partnerships with influencers like Cardi B and Kylie Jenner, who showcased the brand's affordable, body-conscious styles to millions of fans.

E-commerce platforms further accelerated the integration of digital and fashion. Websites like ASOS and Boohoo thrived by combining fast fashion with an intuitive online shopping experience. Features like customer reviews, user-uploaded photos, and personalized recommendations mimicked the social aspects of shopping in physical stores. The rise of mobile commerce made buying even easier, with platforms like Instagram and TikTok integrating shopping features directly into their apps.

TikTok emerged in the late 2010s as a powerful driver of fashion trends. The platform's short, engaging videos often showcased specific items or styles, leading to viral moments that could catapult a brand or trend into the mainstream overnight. Challenges like the #GucciModelChallenge or viral hacks for styling thrifted clothing highlighted TikTok's ability to influence consumer behavior, particularly among Gen Z.

The global reach of digital platforms introduced new levels of inclusivity and diversity to fashion. Influencers from underrepresented communities used social media to showcase their styles, challenging traditional beauty standards and broadening the industry's definition of fashion. Platforms like Instagram became spaces for plus-size, LGBTQ+, and non-Western creators to share their perspectives, fostering a more inclusive fashion landscape.

Digital innovation also fueled the rise of **direct-to-consumer brands**, which bypassed traditional retail models to sell directly through their websites or social media. Companies like Everlane and Glossier used transparency, minimalist aesthetics, and influencer marketing to build loyal followings. These brands thrived on their ability to connect with consumers through storytelling and personalized experiences.

The shift toward digital fashion consumption had significant implications for retail. Brick-and-mortar stores struggled to compete with the convenience and variety offered online. Many brands invested in hybrid models, combining physical stores with robust e-commerce platforms. Pop-up shops and experiential retail spaces emerged as ways to create buzz and connect with digital-first audiences in real life.

Sustainability and ethical concerns also shaped digital fashion trends. Influencers and activists used their platforms to expose fast fashion's environmental and labor abuses, encouraging consumers to rethink their habits. Secondhand marketplaces like Depop and Poshmark gained popularity, particularly among younger consumers, who embraced vintage and upcycled clothing as stylish and sustainable alternatives.

Digital tools also transformed fashion design and production. Brands used **3D modeling and virtual sampling** to reduce waste, while augmented reality allowed consumers to "try on" clothing or accessories virtually. Virtual fashion shows, accelerated by the COVID-19 pandemic, demonstrated how technology could replicate—or even enhance—the traditional runway experience.

The rise of NFTs (non-fungible tokens) in the 2020s introduced a new frontier for fashion. Digital-only garments, sold as NFTs, gained traction among tech-savvy consumers. Brands like Balenciaga and Gucci experimented with virtual fashion, highlighting the growing intersection of fashion and the metaverse. These innovations suggested that the future of style might exist beyond physical garments.

The digital era made fashion more interactive, inclusive, and fast-paced than ever before. By breaking down barriers between brands and consumers, it reshaped the industry into a space driven by community, collaboration, and constant innovation. Influencers, platforms, and technology have permanently altered the way fashion is experienced, making it a dynamic and ever-evolving landscape.

The Intersection of Gender Neutrality and Style

The 21st century has seen a profound shift in how fashion intersects with gender, as traditional boundaries between men's and women's clothing have increasingly blurred. The **rise of gender neutrality in style** reflects broader cultural changes, driven by conversations about identity, inclusivity, and self-expression. This evolution in fashion challenges historical norms, offering individuals the freedom to dress authentically without conforming to predefined categories.

Androgynous fashion, which gained traction in the late 20th century, became a central force in the 21st century. Designers like **Ann Demeulemeester**, **Raf Simons**, and **Rick Owens** championed minimalistic, unisex designs that disregarded traditional gender markers. Their collections often featured neutral color palettes, tailored suits, oversized silhouettes, and garments that could seamlessly fit any body. This approach resonated with a younger generation that valued individuality over binary labels.

The push for gender-neutral clothing gained momentum as the fashion industry embraced **inclusivity in runway shows and campaigns**. Brands like Gucci, under creative director Alessandro Michele, redefined luxury by incorporating androgynous designs into their collections. Models in lace blouses, velvet suits, and flowing gowns walked the runway without consideration for whether the garments were traditionally "masculine" or "feminine." These designs did not just appeal to one gender—they represented a collective statement about fluidity and freedom in fashion.

Retail followed suit, with many brands adopting **gender-neutral lines and spaces**. In 2015, Zara launched its "Ungendered" collection, a line of minimalist T-shirts, sweatshirts, and jeans marketed to all. Similarly, high-street brands like H&M and ASOS began offering collections with relaxed fits, muted tones, and unisex cuts. Even department stores began redesigning their layouts, moving away from strictly divided "men's" and "women's" sections toward unified, inclusive spaces.

Streetwear became a driving force behind the popularity of gender-neutral fashion. Rooted in oversized hoodies, joggers, and sneakers, streetwear's inherently unisex aesthetic aligned perfectly with the demand for non-binary clothing. Brands like Supreme, Off-White, and Fear of God embraced this trend, creating garments that appealed across genders while prioritizing comfort and style. The success of these brands demonstrated that consumers were ready for clothing that didn't adhere to traditional categories.

Pop culture also was influential in normalizing gender-neutral style. Celebrities like Harry Styles, Jaden Smith, and Billie Eilish became icons of fluid fashion, wearing skirts, dresses, and oversized suits unapologetically. Styles' appearance in a Gucci gown on the cover of *Vogue* in 2020 made headlines worldwide, sparking discussions about masculinity, femininity, and the freedom to express oneself through clothing. These public figures challenged stereotypes and inspired fans to experiment with their own wardrobes.

The influence of **social media** amplified the reach of gender-neutral fashion. Platforms like Instagram and TikTok allowed individuals to showcase their personal styles, often blending elements from men's and women's fashion. Influencers and content creators with non-binary or genderqueer identities gained visibility, helping to normalize clothing choices that defied traditional categories. Social media also fostered conversations about the limitations of binary fashion, pushing brands to innovate and expand their offerings.

In tandem with these cultural shifts, **designers began exploring the historical roots of gender-neutral clothing**. Many noted that the strict division between men's and women's clothing is a relatively modern phenomenon. For centuries, garments like robes, tunics, and even heels were worn by people of all genders. Designers drew inspiration from these histories, creating collections that blended masculine and feminine elements in innovative ways.

The rise of **technology and customization** further advanced gender-neutral fashion. Virtual fitting rooms, augmented reality, and AI-driven design tools allowed consumers to explore styles without the constraints of traditional sizing or labels. Brands like Nike introduced sneaker lines designed for all genders, focusing on fit and performance rather than marketing specific styles to men or women. These innovations gave individuals more control over their shopping experiences, empowering them to choose what felt authentic.

Gender-neutral fashion also addressed issues of **body inclusivity**, recognizing that binary sizing systems often excluded those who didn't fit conventional molds. Brands began offering extended size ranges and adaptive clothing that prioritized function over formality. Uniqlo, for instance, emphasized versatility and comfort in its collections, offering pieces designed to fit a wide range of body types without relying on gendered patterns.

Luxury fashion houses increasingly embraced **gender-fluid campaigns**, featuring models of diverse identities wearing clothing that transcended binary definitions. Louis Vuitton cast Jaden Smith in its women's campaign in 2016, where he posed in skirts and floral jackets. Balenciaga and Prada followed with similar campaigns, presenting a vision of style that emphasized individuality rather than conformity. These efforts signaled a shift in how the fashion industry approached storytelling and representation.

The demand for gender-neutral fashion also intersected with the **sustainability movement**, as consumers sought versatile, long-lasting pieces. Capsule wardrobes, which focus on a limited number of interchangeable items, became popular for their practicality and reduced environmental impact. Gender-neutral clothing, with its focus on timeless designs and adaptable fits, aligned perfectly with this trend. Brands like Telfar and Studio Nicholson created collections that prioritized simplicity and quality, appealing to those seeking fewer but better garments.

The push for inclusivity extended to the language surrounding fashion. Terms like "unisex" and "androgynous" evolved into "gender-neutral" and "gender-fluid," reflecting a deeper understanding of identity. Brands began labeling items as "for everyone" rather than "men's" or "women's," emphasizing that clothing was about choice, not prescription. This shift in language demonstrated how the industry was adapting to cultural changes while promoting a more inclusive narrative.

Runways, once dominated by binary models, began featuring a diverse array of talent, including non-binary and transgender individuals. Models like Alok Vaid-Menon and Indya Moore became prominent voices in the movement, advocating for an industry that reflected the realities of modern identity. Their presence on global stages challenged the notion that fashion needed to adhere to outdated conventions.

Critics of gender-neutral fashion pointed out the risk of homogenization, arguing that true freedom in clothing meant celebrating a spectrum of styles, from hyper-feminine to hyper-masculine and everything in between. This debate sparked deeper conversations about the future of fashion, highlighting the need for balance between inclusivity and individuality.

Gender neutrality in fashion redefined how people approached style in the 21st century. It broke down barriers, encouraged innovation, and fostered a culture of self-expression that prioritized authenticity over tradition. By embracing fluidity, the fashion industry moved closer to a future where clothing is truly for everyone.

CHAPTER 16: THE FUTURE OF FASHION

Technological Innovations in Fabric and Design

Technological innovations in fabric and design are reshaping the future of fashion, transforming how clothing is created, worn, and experienced. Advances in materials science, digital tools, and manufacturing processes have pushed the boundaries of what's possible, introducing functionality, sustainability, and interactivity into garments in ways that were once unimaginable. These innovations don't just enhance performance—they redefine the relationship between fashion, technology, and the human body.

Smart textiles are at the forefront of this revolution. These fabrics integrate technology to perform functions beyond traditional clothing, such as monitoring body temperature, tracking physical activity, or even providing light. **Conductive threads** made from materials like silver or carbon allow garments to connect with electronic devices. Companies like Google and Levi's collaborated on the **Jacquard project**, creating a denim jacket embedded with touch-sensitive fibers that can control a smartphone, blending fashion with utility seamlessly.

Wearable technology has moved beyond accessories like smartwatches into fully integrated garments. Designers are incorporating sensors and flexible circuits into clothing, offering features like **health monitoring** and **adaptive fit**. Sportswear brands, for instance, are using smart fabrics to measure heart rate, muscle activity, and hydration levels, giving athletes real-time feedback during training. This fusion of fashion and fitness enhances performance while maintaining comfort and style.

3D printing has transformed how garments are conceptualized and constructed. Designers can now create intricate, customizable patterns with minimal waste, aligning with the growing demand for sustainable fashion. 3D-printed clothing allows for precise control over shape, texture, and structure, enabling innovations like zero-seam garments or pieces that adapt to the wearer's body. Dutch designer Iris van Herpen has pioneered this field, crafting avant-garde collections that blend artistry and technology, showcasing the potential of additive manufacturing.

Sustainability is a driving force behind many fabric innovations. **Bio-fabrication** has introduced lab-grown materials like **mycelium leather**, made from mushroom roots, and **bacterial cellulose**, which can mimic the texture of cotton or silk. These alternatives reduce reliance on animal products and traditional farming, which are resource-intensive. Brands like Stella McCartney and Adidas have already embraced these materials, integrating them into their collections and proving their viability for mass production.

Recycling technologies are advancing rapidly, enabling the transformation of textile waste into high-quality fabrics. Companies like Renewcell and Worn Again Technologies break down old garments into fibers that can be spun into new threads, closing the loop on fashion waste. These recycled fabrics, such as **Circulose**, maintain the look and feel of virgin materials while drastically reducing environmental impact. Paired with growing consumer interest in circular fashion, these innovations could revolutionize how clothes are produced and discarded.

Self-healing fabrics are another exciting development. Inspired by biological processes, these materials can repair small tears or cuts when exposed to heat or moisture. Scientists are developing polymers and coatings that respond to external stimuli, extending the lifespan of garments and reducing the need for frequent replacements. This technology has potential applications in both fashion and outdoor wear, where durability is critical.

Adaptive textiles that respond to environmental changes are becoming more sophisticated. Thermochromic fabrics, for example, can change color based on temperature, creating garments that shift hues throughout the day. Similarly, moisture-wicking fabrics have evolved into textiles that actively regulate temperature, keeping the wearer comfortable in extreme conditions. Companies like Columbia Sportswear are integrating these materials into performance gear, offering clothing that works as hard as the wearer.

The rise of **augmented reality (AR)** and **virtual reality (VR)** is influencing fabric design as well. Virtual prototypes allow designers to test patterns, textures, and fits digitally before production, reducing waste and speeding up the design process. AR also enables consumers to try on clothes virtually, providing a more accurate sense of fit and style without the need for physical samples. This shift toward virtual fashion tools is not only convenient but also aligns with sustainability goals.

AI-driven design is changing how fashion collections are developed. Algorithms analyze consumer preferences, body data, and market trends to create garments that are both personalized and practical. Companies like Uniqlo use AI to optimize clothing lines, ensuring that each piece resonates with customer needs. This technology enhances efficiency and reduces overproduction, a key issue in traditional fashion cycles.

Fabric innovation is also addressing the need for improved performance and comfort. **Moisture-absorbing and odor-resistant materials** are becoming standard in activewear, thanks to advances in textile engineering. Fabrics treated with **antimicrobial coatings** inhibit the growth of bacteria, extending the freshness of garments between washes. These properties appeal not only to athletes but also to consumers seeking low-maintenance clothing for everyday use.

Lightweight and durable fabrics are transforming outerwear and sports gear. Materials like Dyneema, known as the world's strongest fiber, offer unparalleled strength without adding bulk. Initially developed for industrial applications, Dyneema is now used in jackets, backpacks, and shoes, offering protection and longevity. Similarly, graphene, a nanomaterial known for its conductivity and strength, is being incorporated into garments to enhance insulation and durability.

Fashion is also venturing into **biodegradable textiles**, which decompose naturally at the end of their life cycle. Fabrics made from algae, soy, or banana fibers are gaining traction, providing sustainable alternatives to synthetics. These innovations address the growing concern over microplastics and the long-term impact of non-biodegradable materials on ecosystems.

The **integration of energy-harvesting fabrics** is another frontier. Researchers are developing textiles embedded with photovoltaic cells that can convert sunlight into electricity. These garments can power small devices like smartphones, offering a sustainable solution for on-the-go energy needs. Such technologies have potential applications in outdoor gear, military uniforms, and even urban fashion.

Customization is becoming increasingly accessible thanks to **digital knitting and weaving technologies**. Machines can now produce garments to exact specifications, creating one-of-a-kind pieces tailored to individual measurements. This approach reduces waste while catering to consumers seeking personalized fashion. Brands like Ministry of Supply use digital knitting to produce seamless garments that fit perfectly and perform optimally.

The future of fashion also includes **digital-only clothing**, which exists solely in virtual spaces. These garments are designed for avatars, social media content, or virtual events, eliminating the need for physical production. Companies like The Fabricant and DressX are leading this charge, offering digital couture that pushes the boundaries of creativity while reducing environmental impact.

Collaboration between industries is driving many of these innovations. Partnerships between tech companies, universities, and fashion houses are accelerating the development of cutting-edge materials. For example, MIT researchers have worked with designers to create **programmable fabrics** that can change shape or stiffness on command, opening possibilities for garments that adapt to the wearer's needs.

The Role of AI and Virtual Fashion

Artificial intelligence (AI) and virtual fashion are redefining how clothing is designed, produced, marketed, and experienced. By integrating AI algorithms and digital platforms into the creative and logistical processes of fashion, the industry is becoming faster, more personalized, and more sustainable. Virtual fashion is expanding the boundaries of style by creating garments that exist solely in digital spaces, changing the way people engage with clothing.

AI is revolutionizing **fashion design** by analyzing vast amounts of data to predict trends and generate new ideas. Algorithms process inputs like consumer preferences, social media trends, and historical styles to suggest patterns, color schemes, and silhouettes. For example, companies like Heuritech use AI to analyze millions of images from social media, helping brands anticipate emerging trends before they hit the mainstream. This data-driven approach reduces guesswork, ensuring that designs align with current consumer desires.

AI-powered **customization platforms** allow brands to offer bespoke clothing at scale. By analyzing individual measurements, style preferences, and even climate data, AI can create garments tailored to the customer's specific needs. Brands like Amazon and Levi's have explored virtual fitting tools that use AI to recommend the perfect size and fit, reducing returns and improving customer satisfaction. This personalization enhances the shopping experience while minimizing waste from unsold inventory.

In production, AI optimizes **supply chains**, ensuring efficiency and sustainability. Predictive analytics help brands determine how much to produce and where to allocate resources, reducing overproduction. AI also improves inventory management, forecasting demand with precision. Zara, for example, uses AI to track consumer behavior and restock popular items in real time, avoiding the pitfalls of surplus stock and markdowns.

Virtual fashion introduces clothing that exists only in digital form, designed for avatars, social media, or augmented reality (AR) environments. These garments eliminate the need for physical production, significantly reducing their environmental impact. Companies like **The Fabricant** specialize in creating digital couture, offering customers the chance to "wear" luxury designs in virtual spaces. These pieces, often sold as NFTs (non-fungible tokens), represent a new frontier in fashion where creativity and technology merge seamlessly.

Augmented reality is enhancing the **retail experience**, allowing customers to "try on" clothes virtually. Brands like Gucci and Burberry have integrated AR features into their apps, enabling users to see how a garment or accessory looks on them without visiting a store. Virtual fitting rooms reduce the need for physical samples and make online shopping more interactive, boosting engagement and conversion rates.

AI also impacts **sustainability in fashion** by streamlining processes and minimizing waste. Machine learning algorithms identify ways to cut inefficiencies in fabric use and energy consumption during production. Digital prototyping, powered by AI, eliminates the need for physical samples, allowing designers to create and refine collections entirely in virtual spaces before committing to production.

Virtual fashion isn't limited to luxury or gaming—it's becoming part of everyday life. As social media becomes increasingly visual, users are turning to digital fashion to showcase unique styles without purchasing physical garments. Apps like DressX allow users to upload photos and "wear" digital outfits, making bold fashion statements without contributing to textile waste.

AI is also changing how brands market their products. Algorithms analyze consumer behavior to deliver personalized recommendations and targeted advertisements. Chatbots powered by natural language processing provide instant customer support, enhancing the online shopping experience. Virtual stylists, driven by AI, offer curated outfit suggestions based on individual tastes, blurring the line between technology and traditional fashion advice.

Gaming has further fueled interest in AI and virtual fashion. As more people spend time in digital environments, their avatars require clothing that reflects their personalities and tastes. Brands like Balenciaga and Nike have begun creating digital collections for gaming platforms and virtual worlds, tapping into this growing market. These collaborations demonstrate how fashion is expanding beyond physical reality into immersive, interactive spaces.

Predictions for Emerging Trends

The future of fashion will be shaped by a combination of technological innovation, cultural shifts, and environmental imperatives. As the industry continues to evolve, new trends are emerging that will redefine how people interact with clothing, from production to consumption.

AI-driven personalization will dominate the fashion landscape. Consumers increasingly expect clothing that reflects their unique preferences and fits perfectly. Brands will invest in virtual fitting rooms and AI-powered design tools to offer hyper-customized garments. Tailored experiences will become the norm, with algorithms suggesting styles based on body data, climate, and personal taste. This shift will make fashion more inclusive, catering to a diverse range of body types and identities.

The **metaverse** will transform how fashion is consumed. Virtual reality platforms will become mainstream spaces for shopping, socializing, and self-expression. Brands will create digital storefronts in these environments, allowing users to browse and purchase both physical and virtual garments. Avatars will drive demand for digital clothing, with consumers willing to pay for unique, NFT-based designs. These virtual pieces will carry prestige and exclusivity, much like luxury items in the physical world.

Sustainability will remain a central focus, pushing brands to adopt innovative practices. Circular fashion will expand, with increased emphasis on recycling and upcycling. Companies will use advanced textile recycling technologies to convert old garments into high-quality fabrics for new collections. Consumers will embrace rental services and resale platforms as sustainable alternatives to traditional shopping. Digital fashion will also grow, allowing users to wear bold designs without contributing to waste.

The rise of **bioengineered materials** will reshape how clothes are made. Fabrics grown in labs, such as spider silk or mycelium leather, will become widely available, offering sustainable alternatives to conventional textiles. These materials will not only reduce the environmental impact of production but also introduce new possibilities for design. Self-healing fabrics and adaptive textiles, capable of changing shape or color, will revolutionize performance wear and everyday clothing.

The integration of **wearable technology** will advance, making clothing more functional and interactive. Smart garments will monitor health, track fitness goals, and provide real-time feedback. Thermoregulating fabrics, powered by embedded sensors, will adjust to the wearer's body temperature. Solar-powered clothing will gain traction, allowing users to charge devices on the go. These innovations will blend fashion with practicality, offering solutions for modern lifestyles.

Cultural shifts will influence the aesthetics of fashion. Gender neutrality will continue to shape design, with more brands embracing fluid collections that cater to all identities. Inclusivity will extend beyond gender to address size, ability, and age, ensuring that fashion serves a broader audience. Globalization will introduce new influences, with designers drawing inspiration from diverse cultures and traditions, creating a rich tapestry of styles.

The **retail experience** will evolve to prioritize interactivity and convenience. Pop-up shops and immersive events will create buzz and draw consumers into physical spaces, while e-commerce platforms will integrate augmented reality for virtual try-ons. AI-driven chatbots and virtual stylists will make online shopping seamless, offering real-time advice and personalized recommendations.

Artificial intelligence will enhance every stage of fashion production. Predictive analytics will enable brands to anticipate trends with precision, reducing waste and ensuring efficient supply chains. AI-generated designs will become more sophisticated, allowing for rapid prototyping and creative experimentation. These tools will empower both established designers and independent creators, democratizing access to innovation.

Social media will continue to shape trends, with platforms like TikTok driving micro-trends that can emerge and fade within weeks. Influencers will adapt to this fast-paced environment, showcasing new styles and products in real-time. User-generated content will have a larger role, with brands encouraging consumers to share their looks and contribute to trend creation.

The intersection of **technology and craftsmanship** will define the next era of fashion. While digital tools enable precision and efficiency, there will also be a renewed appreciation for traditional techniques and artisanal quality.

Fashion in the future will be a blend of innovation, sustainability, and inclusivity, pushing the boundaries of what clothing can do while staying connected to its cultural roots. These emerging trends suggest an industry that is more dynamic, diverse, and conscious than ever before.

APPENDIX

Timeline of Major Fashion Moments Through History

This timeline highlights how fashion has continuously evolved, shaped by cultural, technological, and societal changes throughout history. Each era introduced innovations and styles that reflected the values and needs of the time while influencing the future of fashion.

Ancient History
3100 BCE - 30 BCE (Ancient Egypt):
- Linen, made from flax, became the primary textile, suited to Egypt's hot climate.
- Men and women wore simple garments like **kilts** and **sheath dresses**.
- Fashion reflected social hierarchy: pharaohs adorned themselves with gold, intricate jewelry, and wigs.

2000 BCE - 1400 BCE (Minoan Civilization):
- Women wore tiered skirts with fitted bodices, emphasizing the waist.
- Snakes, a religious symbol, appeared in jewelry and ceremonial clothing.

1200 BCE - 146 BCE (Ancient Greece):
- The **chiton** and **himation** were common garments, draped and pinned from rectangular cloths.
- Greek fashion highlighted simplicity, symmetry, and functionality, echoing their philosophy of balance.

753 BCE - 476 CE (Ancient Rome):
- Roman fashion adapted Greek styles but introduced the **toga** as a status symbol.
- Textile dyes and intricate embroidery denoted wealth.
- Roman women's **stola** and **palla** reflected modesty and class.

Medieval Period (5th - 15th Century)
400s - 900s (Dark Ages):
- Practicality dominated fashion; people wore tunics, cloaks, and leggings.
- Materials were coarse, often wool or linen, with muted colors.

1000s - 1200s:
- The Crusades introduced Europeans to silks and patterns from the Middle East.
- Romanesque styles favored long, flowing gowns with wide sleeves.

1300s - 1400s (Gothic Period):
- The **houppelande**, a voluminous outer garment, became popular.
- Pointed shoes called **poulaines** symbolized status.
- Women's gowns featured tight bodices and long trains.

Renaissance (15th - 17th Century)

1400s - 1500s:
- Fashion reflected wealth and status; silks, velvets, and brocades became widely used.
- Italian Renaissance clothing featured square necklines and decorative sleeves.
- The **codpiece**, an exaggerated male fashion statement, emerged.

1550s - 1600s:
- The Spanish introduced the **farthingale**, a stiffened underskirt that expanded the gown's shape.
- Elizabethan England embraced ruffs and highly embroidered fabrics.

Baroque and Rococo (17th - 18th Century)

1600s (Baroque):
- Fashion became more extravagant, with lace collars and puffed sleeves.
- Men's fashion featured doublets, breeches, and thigh-high boots.
- The French court of Louis XIV set trends, emphasizing opulence.

1700s (Rococo):
- Women wore **panniers**, wide understructures that created dramatic silhouettes.
- Men adopted **waistcoats** and powdered wigs.
- Pastel colors, floral patterns, and elaborate embroidery defined the era.

Industrial Revolution (Late 18th - 19th Century)

1780s - 1800s:
- Post-Revolution France introduced the simpler **Empire waist gown**, influenced by Greco-Roman styles.
- Men's clothing became more subdued, with trousers replacing breeches.

1820s - 1830s (Romantic Era):
- Women's dresses emphasized femininity with puffed sleeves and fuller skirts.
- Corsetry tightened waists to create the ideal hourglass figure.

1840s - 1860s (Victorian Period):
- Crinolines, made of steel hoops, widened skirts dramatically.

- Mourning fashion gained prominence after Queen Victoria's prolonged mourning for Prince Albert.

1870s - 1890s:
- The bustle replaced crinolines, creating volume at the back of skirts.
- Men's clothing standardized with tailored suits and bowler hats.

Early 20th Century (1900 - 1945)

1900s (Edwardian Era):
- The **S-bend corset** created a dramatic silhouette with a pushed-forward bust and curved back.
- Lace and pastel hues dominated women's clothing.

1910s:
- World War I simplified fashion; hemlines rose for practicality.
- The **hobble skirt**, which restricted movement, reflected a mix of innovation and impracticality.

1920s (The Jazz Age):
- Flapper dresses symbolized liberation, featuring dropped waists and fringe.
- Chanel popularized **boyish silhouettes** and functional elegance.

1930s:
- Bias-cut gowns by designers like Madeleine Vionnet introduced fluid, body-skimming styles.
- The Great Depression brought more subdued, practical clothing.

1940s:
- World War II ushered in **utility fashion**: functional, minimalist designs with limited fabrics.
- Post-war, Dior's **New Look** reintroduced luxury with cinched waists and full skirts.

Mid-20th Century (1950 - 1970)

1950s:
- Hourglass figures defined women's fashion, with circle skirts and fitted bodices.
- Men's fashion leaned toward gray flannel suits, reflecting corporate culture.
- Youth culture emerged with rockabilly looks, leather jackets, and jeans.

1960s:
- The **mod movement** in London introduced miniskirts and bold, geometric patterns.
- Hippie fashion rejected consumerism, embracing ethnic influences and natural fabrics.

1970s:

- Disco inspired glittering fabrics, platform shoes, and wrap dresses.
- Punk fashion emerged as a rebellious counterpoint, with ripped clothing, studs, and leather.

Late 20th Century (1980 - 1999)

1980s:
- Power dressing, epitomized by shoulder pads and tailored suits, reflected ambition.
- Streetwear gained traction, with brands like Adidas and Nike becoming staples.
- Bright neon, oversized silhouettes, and denim defined casual wear.

1990s:
- Minimalism dominated, with designers like Calvin Klein favoring clean lines and neutral palettes.
- Grunge fashion, inspired by the Seattle music scene, featured flannel shirts, ripped jeans, and combat boots.
- The rise of supermodels like Naomi Campbell and Kate Moss influenced high fashion.

21st Century (2000 - Present)

2000s:
- Fast fashion brands like Zara and H&M transformed the industry with rapid production cycles.
- Y2K aesthetics featured metallics, low-rise jeans, and logomania.
- Reality TV and celebrity culture influenced trends.

2010s:
- Athleisure blurred the lines between activewear and everyday fashion.
- Sustainability entered mainstream consciousness, with brands emphasizing eco-friendly practices.
- Streetwear dominated, driven by collaborations between high fashion and sneaker culture.

2020s:
- Virtual fashion emerged, with NFTs and digital garments gaining popularity.
- Gender-neutral collections redefined inclusivity in fashion.
- The pandemic accelerated loungewear trends and shifted focus to comfort and adaptability.

Terms and Definitions

- **A-line Dress**: A dress that is fitted at the waist and gradually widens to form the shape of an "A." Popularized by Christian Dior in the 1950s.
- **Avant-garde**: Experimental or innovative fashion that challenges conventional norms.
- **Baroque Style**: A 17th-century fashion style characterized by opulence, elaborate decoration, and luxurious fabrics like brocade and velvet.
- **Bias Cut**: A technique where fabric is cut diagonally to create garments that cling and drape to the body, made famous by Madeleine Vionnet in the 1920s.
- **Bloomers**: Loose-fitting trousers gathered at the ankle, introduced in the mid-19th century as a more practical alternative to heavy skirts.
- **Bodice**: The upper part of a garment that covers the torso, often fitted or boned in historical fashion.
- **Boho (Bohemian)**: A free-spirited style inspired by the 1960s and 1970s, incorporating elements like fringe, embroidery, and flowing fabrics.
- **Bustle**: A padded or structured undergarment worn in the late 19th century to create volume at the back of a skirt.
- **Chemise**: A simple, loose-fitting undergarment or dress dating back to the Middle Ages.
- **Chiton**: An ancient Greek garment made from a single piece of fabric draped and fastened with pins.
- **Cinch Belt**: A wide belt worn at the waist to create an hourglass silhouette, popular in the 1950s.
- **Cloche Hat**: A close-fitting, bell-shaped hat popular in the 1920s.
- **Corset**: A fitted undergarment with boning, designed to shape and support the torso, used extensively from the Renaissance to the early 20th century.
- **Crinoline**: A stiffened or hooped petticoat worn in the mid-19th century to create a wide skirt.
- **Culottes**: Skirt-like trousers that combine the appearance of a skirt with the functionality of pants.
- **Dandy**: A style associated with men in the late 18th and early 19th centuries, emphasizing refined and elegant clothing.
- **Doublet**: A fitted jacket worn by men in the 14th to 17th centuries.
- **Empire Waist**: A dress style with a high waistline just below the bust, popular in the early 19th century.
- **Epaulettes**: Ornamental shoulder decorations on military uniforms, also influencing civilian fashion.
- **Ephemera**: Fashion items produced for temporary use, such as paper dresses popular in the 1960s.
- **Flapper**: A 1920s fashion icon characterized by short dresses, bobbed hair, and a liberated lifestyle.
- **Gibson Girl**: A fashionable archetype of the late 19th and early 20th centuries, epitomizing elegance and athleticism.
- **Haute Couture**: High-end, custom-fitted fashion produced by exclusive design houses in Paris.
- **Hobble Skirt**: A restrictive skirt that narrows at the hem, popular in the early 1910s.

- **Jacquard**: A fabric with intricate patterns woven into it, created using a specialized loom invented in 1801.
- **Kirtle**: A medieval and Renaissance gown worn by women, often layered with other garments.
- **Kimono**: A traditional Japanese garment with wide sleeves and a wrap-around design.
- **Leg-of-Mutton Sleeves**: Sleeves that are wide and puffed at the top and taper toward the wrist, popular in the Victorian era.
- **Le Smoking**: A tuxedo-style suit for women, introduced by Yves Saint Laurent in 1966.
- **Madras**: A lightweight cotton fabric with a colorful plaid pattern, originating from India.
- **Merry Widow**: A longline strapless corset introduced in the 1950s to create a smooth silhouette.
- **Midi Skirt**: A skirt with a hemline that falls between the knee and ankle, revived in the 1970s.
- **Minimalism**: A style emphasizing simplicity, clean lines, and neutral colors, prominent in the 1990s.
- **Mod Fashion**: A 1960s British youth style featuring bold colors, short hemlines, and geometric patterns.
- **Mutton Chop**: A 19th-century style of facial hair that influenced men's fashion aesthetics.
- **New Look**: A post-World War II style by Christian Dior featuring cinched waists and full skirts, introduced in 1947.
- **Panniers**: Side hoops worn under skirts in the 18th century to create a wide silhouette.
- **Pea Coat**: A short, double-breasted wool jacket worn by sailors and adapted into civilian fashion.
- **Peasant Blouse**: A loose, embroidered top inspired by traditional Eastern European clothing.
- **Petticoat**: An undergarment worn beneath a skirt or dress for volume or warmth.
- **Plaid**: A patterned fabric featuring crisscrossed horizontal and vertical bands, associated with Scottish tartans.
- **Pouf Sleeve**: A rounded, voluminous sleeve, often used in romantic and historical designs.
- **Prince Albert Coat**: A double-breasted frock coat named after Queen Victoria's husband.
- **Punk Fashion**: A rebellious 1970s style featuring ripped clothing, leather jackets, and studded accessories.
- **Renaissance Fashion**: A period of elaborate, ornate clothing characterized by brocade fabrics, ruffles, and rich colors.
- **Romanticism**: A fashion style of the early 19th century inspired by romantic literature and emphasizing flowing, delicate silhouettes.
- **Sack Dress**: A loose, shapeless dress popular in the 1950s and revived in modern minimalist fashion.
- **Safari Jacket**: A belted, lightweight jacket with multiple pockets, inspired by 19th-century colonial attire.

- **Sari**: A traditional South Asian garment made of a long piece of fabric draped around the body.
- **Shift Dress**: A simple, straight-cut dress that hangs loosely from the shoulders, popular in the 1960s.
- **Spats**: Short gaiters worn over shoes, popular in the late 19th and early 20th centuries.
- **Stays**: A type of corset worn in the 16th and 17th centuries for shaping the torso.
- **Stiletto**: A high-heeled shoe with a thin, pointed heel, first popularized in the 1950s.
- **Swing Coat**: A voluminous, A-line coat that flares from the shoulders, popular in the 1950s.
- **Tea Gown**: A casual, loose-fitting dress worn by women in the late 19th and early 20th centuries.
- **Toga**: A draped garment worn in ancient Rome, symbolizing status and citizenship.
- **Trench Coat**: A water-resistant coat developed during World War I, later adopted as a fashion staple.
- **Tunic**: A simple garment worn over the body, common in ancient and medieval fashion.
- **Tuxedo Dress**: A dress inspired by the tuxedo, blending masculine and feminine elements.
- **Velvet**: A soft, luxurious fabric with a dense pile, historically associated with royalty.
- **Victorian Fashion**: 19th-century clothing characterized by corsets, bustles, and elaborate details.
- **Waistcoat**: A sleeveless garment worn over a shirt and under a jacket, part of traditional men's suits.
- **Wasp Waist**: An extremely cinched waist achieved through corsetry, popular in the late 19th century.
- **Weave**: The method of interlacing threads to create fabric, with different techniques producing distinct textures.
- **Yoke**: A fitted part of a garment, such as a shirt or dress, that sits across the shoulders or hips.
- **Zoot Suit**: A 1940s men's suit with exaggerated proportions, including wide shoulders and tapered trousers, popular in jazz culture.

AFTERWORD

As we come to the end of our look through the history of fashion, I hope you've found this book to be more than a collection of facts—it's a story about humanity itself. Fashion is woven into every aspect of our lives, shaping and reflecting who we are as individuals and as a society. It tells tales of creativity, resilience, rebellion, and transformation.

From the earliest scraps of fabric used for protection to the dazzling innovations of modern-day couture, fashion has always been a mirror of its time. It's fascinating to see how trends rise and fall, how societal norms are challenged through clothing, and how something as simple as what we wear can carry such profound meaning.

One of the most enduring lessons from this exploration is that fashion is cyclical. What was once considered cutting-edge becomes nostalgic, only to re-emerge in a new light years later. Yet, while styles may repeat, the context in which they reappear is always different, shaped by the needs and values of the present.

As we look to the future, fashion holds tremendous potential—not just as a medium for artistic expression but as a tool for change. Innovations in technology, sustainability, and inclusivity are transforming the industry. Smart textiles, eco-friendly materials, and virtual fashion are not just trends; they're glimpses of a world where fashion can be both beautiful and responsible. It's an exciting time to be part of this evolving narrative.

But amidst all the change, one thing remains constant: fashion is deeply personal. Whether we use clothing to make a statement, fit in, or stand out, the choices we make each day are uniquely ours. The beauty of fashion lies in its ability to give us a voice without saying a word.

Writing this book has been an incredible experience. Researching, discovering, and connecting the dots between centuries of style has reminded me how much there is to learn from something we often take for granted. My hope is that this book has sparked a similar curiosity in you, inviting you to see the threads of history in your own wardrobe and inspiring you to explore the deeper stories behind the trends you love.

Thank you for joining me on this journey through time, culture, and creativity. Fashion is never static, and neither are we. As the story of style continues to unfold, I encourage you to keep exploring, questioning, and celebrating the unique ways fashion shapes our world.

Until next time—stay curious, stay stylish, and remember, every thread tells a story.

Printed in Great Britain
by Amazon